The Great Compassion

THE GREAT COMPASSION

Buddhism and Animal Rights

NORM PHELPS

LANTERN BOOKS • NEW YORK
A DIVISION OF BOOKLIGHT INC.

2004
Lantern Books
One Union Square West, Suite 201
New York, NY 10003

Printed in the United States of America

Library of Congress Cataloging-in-Publication Data

Phelps, Norm.
The great compassion : Buddhism and animal rights / Norm Phelps.
p. cm.
Includes bibliographical references.
ISBN 1–59056–069–8 (alk. paper)
1. Vegetarianism—Religious aspects—Buddhism. 2. Animal rights—Religious aspects—Buddhism. 3. Compassion—Religious aspects—Buddhism. 4. Buddhist precepts. 5. Ahimsa. I. Title.
BQ4570.V43P54 2004
294.3'5693—dc22
2004005485

Several passages in this book have previously appeared in somewhat different form in the booklet *The Great Compassion: Frequently Asked Questions About Buddhism and Animal Rights*, by Norm Phelps, The Fund for Animals, New York, 2003. Used by permission.

Several passages in Chapter Fourteen and Suggestions for Further Reading have previously appeared in somewhat different form in *The Dominion of Love: Animal Rights According to the Bible* by Norm Phelps, Lantern Books, New York, 2002.

printed on 100% post-consumer waste paper, chlorine-free

ALL BEINGS TREMBLE BEFORE DANGER, ALL FEAR DEATH. WHEN A MAN CONSIDERS THIS, HE DOES NOT KILL OR CAUSE TO KILL.

ALL BEINGS FEAR BEFORE DANGER, LIFE IS DEAR TO ALL. WHEN A MAN CONSIDERS THIS, HE DOES NOT KILL OR CAUSE TO KILL.

HE WHO FOR THE SAKE OF HAPPINESS HURTS OTHERS WHO ALSO WANT HAPPINESS, SHALL NOT HEREAFTER FIND HAPPINESS.

HE WHO FOR THE SAKE OF HAPPINESS DOES NOT HURT OTHERS WHO ALSO WANT HAPPINESS, SHALL HEREAFTER FIND HAPPINESS.

—THE BUDDHA

In memory of
Sandy Lowery
and
Al Skorsch

CONTENTS

ACKNOWLEDGMENTS

Marian Probst, Chair of The Fund for Animals, Michael Markarian, President, and Heidi Prescott, National Director, have been unfailing in their support and encouragement. I have been privileged to work at The Fund for 10 years, and I count this time as the high point of my life, both because of the opportunity that it gives me to be part of an organization that "speaks for those who can't," and the remarkably compassionate people with whom I have had the joy of working. It is in the nature of bodhisattvas that ordinary beings, such as myself, cannot recognize them. But I have absolutely no doubt that I have encountered many at The Fund for Animals and in the animal protection movement generally. Indeed, where would you expect to find bodhisattvas if not among those who are devoting their lives to helping the helpless?

Rynn Berry, Lawrence Carter-Long, Catherine Clyne, Lisa Kemmerer, Andrea Lococo, Michael Markarian, Julia Peirce-Marston, Heidi Prescott, Katherine Purlow, Patti Rogers, Paul Shapiro, Kim Stallwood, Will Tuttle, Paul Waldau, and Eileen Weintraub generously contributed ideas, comments, information, or encouragement that were instrumental to the completion of the manuscript. I am in their debt. Needless to say, responsibility for the final text, including the views expressed and any errors or misstatements, rests entirely with me. I would also like to offer an extra word of thanks to Eileen Weintraub, who graciously provided me with citations and information about vegetarian Tibetan teachers.

There are no words to express my love and admiration for my wife, Patti Rogers, or the magnitude of the difference that she has made in my life. It was she who first encouraged me to study Buddhism and introduced me to animal rights. With every step I take on the spiritual path—and animal rights is certainly a spiritual practice—I find that she has been there ahead of me and is showing me the way. The two spiritual teachers from whom I have learned more than any others are my grandmother, Emma Burton, who taught me in childhood, and Patti, who teaches me in maturity. More recently, a setback in my health has required that she take up far more than her fair share of the labor involved in running a household with a family of rescued cats and a husband with a disability who spends inordinate amounts of time hunched over a computer keyboard. She bears this twin burden with the patience, perseverance, and cheerfulness that can only be found in those in whom abides the great compassion.

Editor, publisher, scholar, essayist, and novelist, Martin Rowe is a person of many gifts, all of which he dedicates to building a just and compassionate society. It has been my extreme good fortune to have the benefit of his guidance and insight in the preparation of this book. Deep appreciation goes also to Sarah Gallogly, editor *extraordinaire* at Lantern Books, who is unfailingly perceptive.

I have been blessed to encounter many compassionate Buddhist teachers. To each of them I am deeply grateful, but especially to the Venerable Lama Kalsang Gyaltsen, spiritual director of Sakya Phuntsok Ling Buddhist Study and Meditation Center in Silver Spring, Maryland, from whom I took my refuge vows and with whom I studied for 12 years.

Norm Phelps
Funkstown, Maryland

INTRODUCTION

Buddhism ought to be an animal rights religion *par excellence*. It teaches the unity of all life; it holds kindness and compassion to be the highest virtues; and it explicitly includes animals in its moral universe. Buddhist rules of conduct—including the First Precept, "Do not kill"—apply to our treatment of animals as well as our treatment of human beings. This would lead us naturally to expect Buddhists to oppose all forms of animal exploitation.

There is, in fact, wide agreement that most forms of animal exploitation are contrary to Buddhist teaching, although crimes against animals are sometimes—inexplicably—treated as minor offenses. Hunting, fishing, animal husbandry, and the use of animals in entertainment are forbidden to Buddhists. But on the question of meat-eating, controversy and confusion reign. Many Buddhists eat meat—although many do not—and monks, priests, and teachers sometimes defend meat-eating as consistent with Buddhist teachings.

Western Buddhists—influenced by a lifetime of the most animal-intensive diet the world has ever known—are especially creative in fashioning Buddhist rationales to justify their addiction to meat, eggs, and dairy. In 1994, in a forum on meat-eating published in *Tricycle*, a popular Buddhist magazine, Bodhin Kjolhede, Abbot of the American Zen Center in Rochester, New York, and dharma heir to Roshi Philip Kapleau, viewed with dismay these efforts to use the Buddhadharma to rationalize meat-eating. "It is sad to see how many American Buddhists are managing to find a self-satisfying accommodation to eating meat. Some airily cite the doctrine of Emptiness, insisting that ultimately there is no killing and no sentient being being killed. Others find cover behind the excuse that taking life is the natural order of things and, after all, 'the life of a carrot and the life of a cow are equal.' "[1] Most of his fellow contributors used the forum to promote precisely the kinds of accommodation to which Kjolhede objected.

This is a critical moment in the history of Buddhism. The next great Buddhist manifestation, Western Buddhism, is still in its formative stage. It has not yet ossified into an orthodoxy that brooks no dissent. There is still time to reject these "self-satisfying accommodations" and tie ourselves firmly to the ethical foundation of the Buddhadharma: boundless compassion for all sentient beings. And it is vital that we do so. Buddhism cannot be true to itself until Buddhists resolve their ambivalence toward nonhuman animals and extend the full protection of their compassion to the most harmless and helpless of those who live at our mercy in the visible realms.

. . .

The Great Compassion grew out of a deep conviction that the Buddhadharma calls upon all of us who take refuge in the Triple Gem not to abandon those beings whose suffering and death may somehow benefit us. It is a feeble compassion that pulls up short where self-interest begins. *The Great Compassion* is also intended for animal protection advocates who wish to take part in a dialogue with members of the Buddhist community. It is, therefore, a book about why—once we have put aside the very appetites and customs that Buddhist practice is intended to help us overcome—the Buddha's teaching leads us to the realization that we must always strive to harm no sentient being, human or nonhuman, whether or not it is in our selfish interests to do so.

. . .

Buddhist ethics are not a legalistic system that allows us to justify behavior on the basis of loopholes, technicalities, or a strict construction of the text. Buddhist ethics are based on motivation and intent. An ethical act is one that is driven by love and compassion and guided by the desire to do the least harm possible to any living being in whatever circumstance we find ourselves. An unethical act is one that is driven by craving, fear, or anger and guided by the desire to benefit ourselves by harming another living being. Thinking like a lawyer or an academic logician and claiming that it is acceptable to harm another sentient being for our own selfish benefit based on hair-splitting distinctions and nimble logic is contrary to the teaching of the Buddha.

After noting that "Ethical conduct (*sila*) is built on the vast conception of universal love and compassion for all beings, on which the Buddha's teaching is based," the Venerable Walpola Rahula, a monk, university professor and social activist who was one of the twentieth century's leading exponents of Theravada Buddhism, observes, "It is regrettable that many scholars forget this great ideal of the Buddha's teaching and indulge in only dry philosophical and metaphysical divagations when they talk and write about Buddhism. The Buddha gave his teaching 'for the good of the many, for the happiness of the many, out of compassion for the world.'"[2]

A trend in contemporary Western Buddhism that is just as pernicious is the growing tendency to treat the Buddha as just

XVI / THE GREAT COMPASSION

another self-help guru, like Wayne Dyer or Dr. Phil, whose lecture series might show up on public television during the pledge drive. According to this school of thought, the purpose of spiritual practice is to reduce stress, lower anxiety, and generally make us better adjusted and less neurotic. Advocates of Buddhism as self-help do not so much deny the importance of compassion as reduce it to a set of mental exercises that fill us with warm fuzzies while having little or no effect on the world around us. The Buddha taught that we cannot achieve our own happiness until we are prepared to sacrifice it for the happiness of others. Buddhist self-help coaches teach that we cannot make others happy until we first make ourselves happy. It is, as the saying goes, a question of priorities.

Most of the discussion about whether Buddhists should eat meat takes place in this kind of moral vacuum. That is to say, it deals exclusively with the mental state of the practitioner and ignores the suffering of the animals. As long as this trend continues, the role of veganism in Buddhist practice will never be properly understood. As a way of placing the discussion that will occupy the bulk of this book in its moral context, the first chapter will consider the scale of the killing that our society carries out, while the second will look at the suffering that we inflict upon farmed animals before we kill them.

. . .

There are two main schools of Buddhism: *Theravada* and *Mahayana*. Sometimes known as the "southern school," Theravada Buddhism is found in Sri Lanka and most of Southeast Asia, including Burma and Thailand. Mahayana, the "northern school," is found in China, Central Asia, Korea, Japan, and Vietnam. Both schools trace their origin to the Indian sage

Siddhartha Gautama (566–486 BCE),³ who was the eldest son of a wealthy and powerful north Indian ruler.

At 29, profoundly disturbed by the universality of sickness, old age, and death, Prince Siddhartha renounced the treasures and pleasures of the world and slipped away from the palace in the dead of night to pursue the path of a mendicant spiritual seeker—leaving behind his father, stepmother, wife, and newborn son.⁴ For six years, he studied with the leading spiritual teachers of his day and practiced the harsh physical austerities that were believed necessary if the will was to gain mastery over the stubbornness and weakness of the flesh. Finally, he was so weakened by hunger that he lost the power of concentration. This convinced him that punishing the body is not the route to enlightenment because the body is the only vehicle we have in which to reach it. This realization led Siddhartha to espouse "the middle way," a balanced approach to living that eschewed equally the extremes of luxury and austerity.

Reinvigorated, he sat down beneath a pipal tree near the town of Gaya in northeastern India, vowing not to arise until he had gained enlightenment. As the night wore on, he sank deeper and deeper into meditative absorption, and finally, just before dawn, achieved his goal. From the Sanskrit word for "enlightenment" or "awakening," Siddhartha became known as the Buddha, the Enlightened One—or, as Huston Smith translates it, "the Man Who Woke Up"—while the town became known as Bodh Gaya and the tree as the Bodhi Tree. At first, the Buddha was inclined to pass directly into the eternal bliss of Nirvana, without sharing his discovery, so convinced was he that trying to teach others the path to enlightenment was a hopeless task. But then he thought, "There will be a few who will understand and will be able to gain release from their suffering." And so, out of compassion, he remained in samsara for another 45 years, teaching, in his own description, "suffering and the end of suffering." He died at the age of 80 and his body was cremated in accordance with Indian custom. The cause of his death will become important when we consider whether the Buddha ate meat.

Like Pythagoras, Socrates, and Jesus, the Buddha wrote nothing down, although he was certainly literate in Sanskrit, the classical literary language of ancient India, and Magadhi, the closely related vernacular of Magadha, modern Bihar, where he spent most of his life. His followers also wrote nothing down, but transmitted his teachings orally for more than 400 years. Finally, the fourth Buddhist Council decided to commit the teachings to writing. The result was the *Pali Canon*, named for the ancient Indian language in which it is written, which is the only scripture accepted by Theravadins. Mahayanists accept the Pali Canon as scripture, but place greater reliance on a separate body of scriptures originally written in Sanskrit—although many texts have survived only in Chinese or Tibetan translations.

Both sets of scriptures are divided into three categories, known as the *Tripitaka*, the "three baskets." The *Vinaya Pitaka* contains the rules of monastic discipline; the *Sutra Pitaka* records the discourses of the Buddha; and the *Abidharma Pitaka* consists of treatises on philosophy and psychology. With occasional exceptions, we will be concerned only with the Sutra Pitaka. Tibetan Buddhists accept a third body of scriptures, also written in Sanskrit, known as the Tantras, but they deal primarily with esoteric meditation techniques and will not concern us much here.

The disagreements between Theravada and Mahayana are actually quite small. Mostly, they involve differing interpretations of ontological and metaphysical questions that have little bearing on the issues we are discussing. On the subjects of compassion and ethics, it is easy to generalize about Buddhism because the teachings of the schools are so completely in agreement.

A Note on Buddhist Vocabulary

Most Buddhist terms exist in two forms, Sanskrit and Pali, although some words, such as *karuna*, "compassion," are the same in both languages. In the body of the text, I will use the more familiar Sanskrit form, e.g., *dharma* instead of *dhamma*, and give the Pali equivalent in the Glossary. When referring to Mahayana scriptures, I will use the Sanskrit word "sutra," and, when referring to Theravadin scriptures, the Pali equivalent, "sutta."

A Note on Buddhist Titles

"Ajahn" is a Thai honorific derived from the Sanskrit *acharya*, "teacher"; it identifies a qualified teacher of Theravada Buddhism. "Bhante" is a Pali honorific that designates a Theravadin abbot or other highly respected teacher. "Bhikkhu" ("monk") is a Pali honorific. The Sanskrit equivalent is "Bhikkshu." "Geshe" is a Tibetan title, most commonly used by the Gelugpa school, that may be considered the rough equivalent of a Ph.D. "Lama" identifies a qualified teacher of Tibetan Buddhism, who may be a monk or a householder. It is the Tibetan translation of the Sanskrit *guru*. "Mahathera" ("Great Elder") is a Pali honorific signifying a fully ordained Theravadin monk who has maintained his vows for at least 20 years. "Rinpoche" ("Precious One") is a Tibetan honorific that usually, but not invariably, identifies the reincarnation of a deceased lama. "Roshi," often translated "Zen Master," is a Japanese honorific indicating that the holder has been authenticated by a senior Zen Master as a qualified teacher of Zen.

"Sayadaw" is a Burmese honorific that designates a Theravadin abbot. "Sensei" ("Teacher," "Mentor") is a Japanese honorific that also designates a teacher of Zen. "Thera" ("Elder") is a Pali honorific signifying a fully ordained Theravadin monk who has maintained his vows for at least 10 years. "Thich" is a Vietnamese honorific indicating a Buddhist monk.

CHAPTER I

THE ROSARY OF DEATH

In the time of the Buddha, a local aristocrat named Kusananji and his wife Mantani had a son whom they named Ahimsaka, "He Who Does No Harm." As a young man, Ahimsaka was devout and studious, and so his parents sent him to Taxila University, one of the finest schools in India. There, he fell under the influence of an evil teacher who told Ahimsaka that if he hoped to gain liberation from samsara he would have to kill a thousand people and create a prayer rosary made from their knuckles.

Much distressed, but trusting his teacher and determined to gain the bliss of liberation, Ahimsaka became a highwayman, waylaying travelers, killing them, and stringing their knuckles onto a gruesome rosary that he wore around his neck. Dreaded by all, he became known as Angulimala, "Finger Rosary."

Early one morning, Angulimala awoke, counted the knuckles on his rosary, and realized that he had killed 999 people. "Today," he said to himself, "I will kill the first person

I see; my task will be accomplished; and the unending bliss of liberation will be mine." By a terrible coincidence, the first person he saw that day was his mother. Blinded by the false teachings he had received, Angulimala rushed at Mantani, meaning to kill her and complete his rosary of death with her knuckle bone.

Fortunately the Buddha, who was on his way into town to beg his daily meal, witnessed this dreadful scene and deliberately walked between Angulimala and his horrified mother. Angered by the effrontery of this unarmed monk, Angulimala turned to attack the Buddha instead. But no matter how hard Angulimala ran, he could never catch up, even though the Buddha continued his stroll toward town at a normal pace.

"Stop!" the frustrated bandit screamed at the Buddha.

"I have stopped," said the Buddha gently, as he continued to walk. "You are the one who hasn't stopped."

"I don't understand," panted an exhausted and exasperated Angulimala. "What do you mean, you've stopped and I haven't?"

"Angulimala, I have stopped completely by abandoning violence against all living beings."

Hearing that, Angulimala understood that the Buddha had ended the painful cycle of rebirth by choosing to live in a way that harmed no living being. He realized that when we inflict suffering on others, we create suffering for ourselves. Our liberation depends on adopting a life of nonviolence. The bandit repented, took refuge vows, and became a follower of the Buddha, a monk known for his gentleness and compassion. "My name is Ahimsaka, 'He Who Does No Harm,' " he said later, "But I used to be 'himsaka,' one who does harm to others. Now, I live up to my name because I harm no living being."[1]

. . .

Like Angulimala, we seek happiness by killing living beings. Our food, our clothing, and our entertainment all come at the price of billions of deaths. Every year in the United States alone,

Ten billion cows, pigs, sheep, goats, chickens, ducks, and turkeys are killed for food and fabric. Of those, nine billion are chickens.[2] Worldwide, 48 billion land animals are killed for food and fabric, of whom 46 billion are chickens, ducks, turkeys, and geese.[3] The number of aquatic animals—primarily fish, lobsters, shrimp, crabs, oysters, and clams—killed for food is not known because production estimates are made in metric tons rather than numbers of animals. In 2001, world fisheries production, both aquaculture and capture, was estimated at just over 130 million metric tons, live weight.[4] A metric ton is 2,205 pounds. If we estimate the weight of the average fish, mollusk, and crustacean at 20 pounds, which is probably high, this would yield a worldwide total of over 14 billion aquatic animals slaughtered every year. The number of silkworms boiled alive each year in the production of silk is not known.

One hundred and fifteen million animals who live in the wild are killed for pleasure.[5] To most Americans, who live in cities and suburbs, sport hunting is all but invisible. They are barely aware that it goes on. And yet, it is the second leading form of animal killing in America.

More than 20 million animals are killed in biomedical research and product testing laboratories.[6] Ninety percent of these are rats and mice, but cats, dogs, rabbits, and primates are also popular research victims. The creation of genetically modified ("transgenic") mice for use in laboratories is now a booming industry. These unfortunate beings are created with a genetic predisposition to contract a specific disease. They are deliberately designed by human beings in order that they may suffer and die from a human-inflicted illness. The recent discovery that the DNA of dogs replicates human DNA more closely than does the DNA of mice will soon lead to the creation of transgenic dogs and a catastrophic increase in the number of dogs who suffer and die in laboratories.

So far, I have counted only the animals whose death is the purpose of their use. But there are millions more who die every year because they are surplus to the need, or they have outlived their usefulness and become an economic liability. We kill them to save the cost of their upkeep. Every year in the United States:

Six to eight million dogs and cats go into the institutions that we euphemistically call "shelters," either because their guardians gave them up or they were found homeless on the street. Most are normal, healthy animals who would love to have a home; and yet more than half of them are killed simply because the number of animals who need homes is so much greater than the number of people who go to shelters to adopt a companion.[7]

An estimated 20,000 racing greyhounds[8] and 40,000 horses,[9] most of whom are "retired" racehorses, are killed because they are too slow or too old to be profitable. This does not include 30,000 horses who are shipped to Canada every year for slaughter and an unknown number who are shipped to Mexico.[10] Horseracing fans may delude themselves that when the animals are no longer able to compete, they are retired to a life of ease on a picturesque farm in blue grass country. But this is true only for the lucky few who can be profitably bred. The vast majority of "retired" American racehorses are sent to slaughter for pet food or for human consumption in Europe.

Unknown numbers of exotic animals from circuses and zoos are "euthanized," sent to slaughter, or sold to canned hunts because there is no room for them or they are no longer paying their way as public attractions.[11]

Even now, we have not counted the billions of animals who are killed accidentally every year. Their individual deaths may not be intentional, but we do little or nothing to reduce the number of victims. We would rather kill them than bear the minimal inconvenience and cost of saving their lives. Every year in the United States:

Three hundred million animals are killed by cars and trucks on our roads and streets.[12] This includes 5.4 million cats and 1.2 million dogs.[13] Many of these animals are not killed immediately, but drag themselves away to die slowly in unseen agony. Simple measures, such as widening the shoulders of roads, installing roadside reflector systems, and equipping new cars with wide-beam headlights—coupled with programs of public education and enforcement similar to those promoting seat belt use and attacking drunk driving—could reduce these deaths dramatically.

Unknown millions of birds and small animals fall victim to high-tech agriculture as they are run over or ground to pieces by massive farm equipment operated by workers perched high atop tractors the size of an army tank.

Millions more birds and small animals, including chipmunks, rabbits, raccoons, opossums, skunks, and moles are killed directly or indirectly by the chemical herbicides, pesticides, and fertilizers that are needed to sustain industrial monocrop agriculture, rapidly proliferating golf courses, and endless suburbs with lawns suitable for *Better Homes and Gardens*.

. . .

Everywhere we turn, we encounter the killing of the harm-

less and the helpless. Our society is soaked through with
killing like a piece of cloth drenched in blood. Our minds
have become so permeated by killing that we do not recognize
it as wrong, even while we are sitting on our cushions generating compassion toward all living beings. Like Angulimala,
we have been persuaded that our happiness is dependent
upon killing. And so with every slice of bacon and every
scrambled egg that we eat, with every glass of milk we drink,
every pair of leather shoes we wear, every silk shirt we put on,
every horse race or circus we attend, we string another finger
bone on our rosary of death. The number of knuckles on
Angulimala's rosary reached 999 and in any event would have
stopped at 1,000. The knuckles on our rosaries are too many
to count, and their number grows without limit.

CHAPTER 2

LIFE ON THE FARM

A t least Angulimala fell upon his victims suddenly and killed them swiftly, with a stroke of the sword. By contrast, the animals we kill, especially those we eat, die terrifying deaths after lives of suffering and deprivation. The modern farm is a sweatshop for animals, and farming today has more in common with the worst excesses of the industrial revolution than with family farming as it persists in our popular folklore.

Until the middle of the last century, farming was based on natural processes. Animals were kept in a loose confinement—a pasture, a field, or a yard—that more or less replicated their natural habitat. To some extent, they were able to live according to their natures: cows, sheep, and goats could graze in the company of their fellows; pigs could forage and root together; and chickens could walk about pecking at bits of roughage on the ground and sleep on roosts that made reasonable substitutes for the trees in which their jungle ancestors slept. Farmers took nature for their model; and if their imitation was less than perfect, by and large, it still provided the animals with at least the most basic comforts and satisfactions that their natures demanded—at least until the time came for slaughter.

In the second half of the twentieth century, this all changed as farmers turned away from nature and began looking to industry as a model for raising animals. This movement had been foreshadowed a hundred years earlier when the Chicago stockyards mechanized the slaughter of cattle, sheep, and pigs. No longer were animals killed individually and personally, so to speak, as if by a natural predator; now they were slaughtered impersonally and *en masse*. The opening of the vast Union Stockyards on Christmas Day, 1865, was the beginning of the end for the natural model of animal agriculture, although it would take a century for the raising of animals to catch up with the killing of them.[1]

Industrial animal agriculture, which the industry calls "intensive confinement animal production" (ICAP) and everyone else calls "factory farming," was ushered in by the invention of chemicals and drugs, especially antibiotics, that made it possible to raise animals under conditions so unnatural that only a heavily medicated animal could survive to slaughter. This opened the door for farming on a scale that was attractive to wealthy corporations. When companies like Tyson and ConAgra began taking over American agriculture in the 1960s, most family farmers could compete only by making a capital investment so large that they had to mortgage their land to finance it. At that point even a small dip in prices on the commodities market meant bankruptcy.

The guiding principle of factory farming is to ratchet up profits by using capital investment to maximize production and minimize time and labor. Trying to run a family farm in the twenty-first century is like trying to compete with GM and Ford by building cars in your garage. It can't be done. And, in fact, it isn't done, at least not on any meaningful scale. Today, family farmers have about the same impact on food production that hobbyists who build their own cars have on automobile production. Unless you shop at a co-op or organic food store—and even that is no guarantee—it is a near certainty that your meat, dairy, and eggs come from a factory farm.

. . .

Howard Lyman describes himself as "a fourth-generation dairy farmer and cattle rancher. I grew up on a dairy farm in Montana," he tells us, "and I ran a feedlot operation there for 20 years. I know firsthand how cattle are raised and how meat is produced in this country."[2] Lyman has this to say about the state of the family farm.

> Family farming in the Montana that I knew is not just dying, as I had feared—it is dead. . . . Competing against agribusinesses, giant feedlots, and megadairies—all of which have taken every advantage of their size and rigged government policy to favor themselves, none of the family farmers truly had a chance. . . . When I sold my farm in 1983, there were about 1,250,000 full-time commercial family farms in America. Today [1998] about 400,000 remain. At this rate, the family farmer will be virtually extinct within a decade.[3]

Speaking of the growth of factory farms to a position of near monopoly in the food market, Matthew Scully, a former literary editor at the *National Review* and current speechwriter for President George W. Bush, says, "Of course small farmers, doing things so much less 'sophisticatedly' than their corporate competitors, cannot survive in this environment."[4]

And this gets us to a significant, but often overlooked, fact of modern life. Farmers who follow the natural model, so-called "free-range" farming, will never be able to provide meat, eggs, and dairy on a large enough scale to feed the American public, much less feed us at prices we will be willing to pay. *The only alternative to factory farms is a vegan America.* Attempts to establish "humane standards" for farming that will permit people to eat animal products with a clear conscience are misguided. They are misguided in a moral sense because they fail to address the ultimate ethical issue: killing for food that we do not need to live—to put it more bluntly, killing for the pleasures of consumption. And they are misguided in a practical sense because "humane" or "free-range" farms will never be able to replace factory farms any more than corner grocery stores will be able to replace supermarkets. Free-range farms require too much land, too much time, and too much labor.

Nostalgia for a kinder, gentler age may be comforting, but we cannot create a better future by trying to re-create a lost past. New circumstances require new solutions. Values are eternal; practices are ephemeral. The solution to the ethical, environmental, and health crises inherent in industrial agriculture is not to try to return to a system of family farms that has no chance of economic survival; it is to create a vegan society. When we buy "organic" meat or "free-range" eggs, we may feel like we are doing the right thing. But, in fact, we are still supporting the factory farming system because we are not moving in the only direction that can save animals from slaughter and the horrors of intensive confinement.

. . .

The industrial model of animal agriculture depends on treating animals as raw materials to be turned into a product as quickly and efficiently as possible. This means showing no more concern for their needs and feelings than if they were pieces of steel or plastic. The industry likes to tell us that happy, healthy animals are better producers than sick, unhappy animals and so it is in the company's interest to provide good living conditions. This is a lie. In fact, the opposite is true. Let's take a look at life on a factory farm.

Home on the Feedlot
According to Jeffrey Moussaieff Masson, psychoanalyst and Freud scholar turned investigator of the emotional lives of animals, most beef cattle "are weaned at six to 10 months of age [nine months to a year is natural], live three to five months on the range, spend four to five months being fattened on a feedlot, and are typically slaughtered at 15 to 20 months. Considering that their average lifespan is nine to 12 years, these animals live only a brief fraction of the time they were meant to live."[5] Your prime rib or Big Mac is the flesh of an adolescent who was just starting out in life.

A feedlot is a large pen, usually but not necessarily outdoors, in which several hundred to several thousand beef cattle are held in conditions of intensive confinement so that they can be fed a special food mixture, including bovine growth hormone (BGH), that will fatten them up quickly. Since the stomachs of cattle are meant to digest grass, the feedlot mixture causes diarrhea and a bevy of other gastric disorders. A typical feedlot holds around 5,000 cattle on about 10 acres of concrete floor, room enough for them to move around, but just barely. Without the concrete paving, the animals would find themselves standing in foot-deep mud every time it rained.

As it is, feedlots are all feces, urine, flies, and the potent chemicals and pesticides that are used to suppress disease under conditions that are pathogen paradise. To keep disease from destroying their herds in a matter of days, feedlot operators have to lace their feed with antibiotics.[6] On the open range, you would find one cow for every 10 to 20 acres of rangeland. In the east, where there is thick grass instead of scrub, you might find a density as high as one cow for every two or three acres. On a feedlot, you find 500 cows per acre. They cannot graze, they cannot roam, they cannot form structured herds—they can do none of the things that it is in the nature of cattle to do.

This Little Pig Went to Market

Pigs are the latest animals to fall under the yoke of industrial agriculture. As recently as 20 years ago, most pigs were still raised on family farms in some loose form of confinement. But no longer. During the 1980s and '90s agribusiness moved in on the family pig farmer in a big way; today huge factory farms holding tens of thousands of pigs in confinement sheds are the industry standard.[7] Needless to say, this high concentration of pigs generates enormous amounts of solid and liquid waste. Industrial pig farms can often be smelled from miles away, and numerous jurisdictions have passed zoning laws banning them, even when other types of agriculture are permitted. Modern pig farms destroy the quality of life of those who live near them—not to mention the value of their property—pollute the groundwater and nearby rivers and streams, and make prime breeding grounds for flies, mosquitoes, and practically every kind of pathogen that can grow in a temperate climate.

. . .

In nature, baby pigs are born in nests of soft straw and leaves lovingly made by their mothers. Factory-farmed pigs come into the world on the concrete floor of a farrowing pen. Farrowing pens and gestation crates are metal cages so narrow—22 inches wide is standard—that the mother pig cannot stand up, roll over, or turn around. She spends her entire adult life lying on her side on hard cement, first in the gestation crate being artificially inseminated and waiting to give birth, then in the farrowing pen having her babies and nursing them. When one family of babies is ready to be weaned, she is taken back to the gestation crate, impregnated again, and the cycle starts anew.[8] After eight pregnancies, she is considered "spent" and sent to slaughter.[9]

Pigs are intelligent, curious, and friendly animals; in personality they are much like dogs. They can be taught, and they enjoy human companionship, although I do not recommend trying to make a companion of one unless you are certain that you have the facilities and resources to care for an animal who may weigh upwards of 500 pounds. Isolation and forced immobility have a devastating effect on both the physical and emotional health of breeding sows. Sores and tumors are commonplace; the pigs lose the ability to stand and walk as joints freeze and muscles atrophy. How painful this must be we can only imagine. Visitors to hog farms report that they can tell by her attitude how long a breeding female has been penned. The new arrivals are restless and aggressive; they struggle to get free and bite at the bars of the cage; long-timers, on the other hand, are depressed, listless, and withdrawn.[10] In the same circumstances, you or I would likely go through the same progression as we spiraled downward into a soul-crushing pit of despair.

. . .

The confinement building to which the pigs are sent when they leave their mother at about three weeks of age is called a "finishing shed." Their lives are defined by concrete floors, cinderblock or metal walls, artificial light, and rank, nasty-smelling air. Most never see sunlight or feel the earth beneath their feet. None will ever be able to run and play, root in the ground, or roll in the mud, all activities that are born into the nature of a pig. Crammed in cheek by jowl with tens of thousands of their fellows, utterly without hope of relief, normally gentle, easygoing pigs turn vicious and begin biting one another's tails. Since this causes infection and lowers production, hog farm operators routinely dock the tails of their pigs, without anesthesia. Among free-ranging pigs, tail biting does not occur; it is a sign that overcrowding and unnatural confinement have driven them insane. They are sent to the slaughterhouse—euphemistically styled a "packing plant"—when they reach 250 pounds, about half of their full adult weight. Like all animals raised for food, they are killed while they are still children.

The Chickens and the Eggs

Karen Davis is a former university professor who left the security of academia to take up the cause of those whom she believed to be the most overlooked of the helpless victims of humanity—chickens and turkeys. Founder and president of United Poultry Concerns, a national advocacy group that also runs a sanctuary in the heart of chicken country on the eastern shore of Virginia, Dr. Davis is a passionate woman with haunting eyes that seem always to be gazing upon the suffering of her beloved birds. An internationally recognized authority on poultry, her harrowing descriptions of how domestic fowl are raised and slaughtered have never been falsified by the poultry industry; in fact, time and again video footage by rescue groups like Compassion Over Killing has verified everything she has said. In *Prisoned Chickens, Poisoned Eggs: An Inside Look at the Modern Poultry Industry*, Davis says that broiler chickens may live on an open floor or in battery cages. On an open floor, they are crowded to such a density that they typically are allowed only 115 square inches per bird, a space about 10 by 12 inches.[11]

Compare this to the fact that a three- to four-pound chicken needs a minimum of 74 square inches merely to stand, 197 square inches to turn, 138 square inches to stretch, 290 square inches to flap wings, 135 square inches to ruffle feathers, 172 square inches to preen, and 133 square inches to scratch the ground. These are basic biological activities.[12]

Chickens in a confinement shed spend their entire lives unable to do the things that they are genetically driven to do. To gain a sense of what this must be like, imagine having to live for years underground on a crowded subway train, people packed in so tightly against one another no one can move more than an inch or two. Turning around or walking a few steps is out of the question.

Laying hens and many broiler chickens get even less space. They live in small wire pens, called battery cages, stacked horizontally and vertically in a confinement shed. A typical battery cage is 12 inches by 18 inches and holds four or five chickens.[13] At best, this works out to 54 square inches of space in which each bird has to live out her life. Whenever we eat an egg, feeling virtuous because we think no animal was killed in its production, we should remember those 54 square inches—a little more than half the size of a sheet of typing paper—that are the only world the hens who lay our eggs ever know.

But overcrowding is only one of the horrors with which factory farmed chickens must live. The poorly ventilated con-

finement sheds are gas chambers, filled with toxic ammonia
from the urine of tens of thousands of chickens.[14] The sheds
are automated to the point that workers have to enter them
only occasionally, but even so asthma, chronic bronchitis, and
emphysema are among the hazards of the occupation.[15] Being
a factory farm worker today is akin to being a coal miner in
the nineteenth century. Do you remember our imaginary subway car? Add a constant fog and stench of eye-watering,
throat-burning, gut-wrenching ammonia from urine. Then
add several layers of cars with wire roofs and floors directly
above yours, so that the urine and feces of the passengers
crammed into them is constantly dropping and dripping
down on you. Now you have a pretty good idea of the suffering that creates fried chicken and scrambled eggs.

The effects of a life lived in these conditions are entirely as
you would expect. Painful and crippling leg and foot deformi-
ties (from living on a wire floor), poor blood circulation,
osteoporosis, fatty liver hemorrhagic syndrome, swollen head
syndrome, salmonella, coccidiosis, and a host of other conditions that are rare in free-range chickens are common in the
confinement shed, making factory chicken farming dependent
on the massive use of antibiotics just to keep the flock from
being wiped out by their living conditions.[16]

Psychologically, the effects of intensive confinement are
just as devastating. Because of severe overcrowding, the
impossibility of organizing a normal social structure (a flock),
and the absence of any opportunity to dustbathe—a behavior
as important to a chicken's emotional well-being as to her
physical health—abnormal, severely neurotic behavior
becomes the norm in confinement sheds. The worst symptom
of this farmer-induced insanity is called "cannibalism," a syndrome in which the overcrowded chickens peck savagely at
one another, inflicting serious damage and even death, behav-

ior unknown in free-ranging chickens. To deal with this, factory farmers routinely "debeak" their chickens, i.e. cut or burn off their beaks, without anesthesia, despite the fact that a chicken's mouth, like yours or mine, is extremely sensitive to pain.[17] And so, to return to our image of the subway car, imagine that just before you were shoved into it, someone had pulled all of your teeth without an anesthetic.

. . .

The cost of eggs in death and suffering does not stop here. As soon as a laying hen is no longer able to produce at a level that is profitable to the farm, she is killed. Since male laying chickens are useless to the industry—they don't grow enough flesh fast enough to make them profitable as broilers—they are killed at birth. Citing the National Agricultural Statistical Service of USDA, Karen Davis tells us that, "In 1995, the U.S. egg industry slaughtered over one million 'spent' laying hens and killed 247 million unwanted male chicks at the hatchery."[18] When we eat eggs we assume responsibility for the killing of a quarter billion chickens every year, not including the uncounted millions who die from the diseases caused by their living conditions.

A White Plague

A cow is not a milk machine. She is a female mammal, and like other female mammals she only lactates when she has been pregnant. To keep a steady supply of milk coming, a cow has to be made pregnant every year of her adult life. And to keep it going to humans who don't need it, the calf who does must be deprived of it. Female calves are typically taken from their mothers a few days after birth; some are fed a milk substitute and eventually turned into dairy cows themselves; others are sold to be slaughtered for beef. Male calves are taken from their mothers almost immediately after birth and confined in cages—known as "veal crates"—so narrow that they cannot lie down, turn around, or lick themselves, the idea being to prevent them from developing muscle tone, which would make the veal less tender. They are then fed a diet completely lacking in iron, which, as you might expect, causes a severe iron deficiency anemia that leaves their muscle tissue white, the color favored by connoisseurs of veal. As anyone who has had anemia knows, it is a debilitating and extremely distressing condition; iron deficiency anemia causes suffering, and severe anemia causes severe suffering. At 15 weeks old, while he is still a baby, the veal calf is sent to slaughter.[19]

Like chickens, dairy cows are kept in a completely controlled environment. Whether they are held indoors on a concrete surface that damages their hooves or outdoors in a small yard that turns to ankle-deep mud when it rains, they are not allowed to graze but are fed a special formula that increases their milk output. Peter Singer notes that:

> The cow's peculiar digestive system cannot adequately process this food. The rumen [one of the four divisions of a cow's stomach] is designed to digest slowly fermenting grass. During peak production, a few weeks after giving birth, the cow expends more energy than she is able to take in. Because her capacity to produce surpasses her ability to metabolize her feed, the cow begins to break down and use her own body tissues.[20]

After five or six years of constant pregnancy, twice-daily milking, and an improper diet, a dairy cow is "spent" and sent off to slaughter. Modern milk production requires the killing of cows as surely as does beef production.

Although the living conditions of dairy cows may not be as horrific as those of chickens, they are still oppressive. Cows are herd animals, and in intensive confinement, dairy cows are unable to be part of a herd, which causes them great stress. On old-fashioned farms, cows bonded with their keepers much as dogs do, but this, too, is impossible on a factory farm. Gregarious social animals by nature, dairy cows live their entire lives in unnatural isolation.

Bovine mothers also have much in common with their human counterparts. "They carry their young for nine months, just as we do, and then they suckle them for between nine and 12 months, like so many human mothers."[21] When their babies are taken away they bellow and moan for days, and have been known to stand gazing at the spot where they last saw their calf for six weeks or longer.[22] Considering these things, Jeffrey Moussaieff Masson asks, "Can anyone doubt that they mourn and grieve and love their children as much as we love ours? Who are we to dismiss with human arrogance the depth or importance of these feelings?"[23] And who are we with human arrogance to *cause* this mourning and this grief for the sake of a slice of cheese or a dish of ice cream?

They Do Not Go Quietly

Animals on factory farms die prematurely of confinement-induced injury or disease; they are killed by fellow inmates stressed to the breaking point: they are sent to slaughter. Except for the occasional individual—among billions—who is rescued by an animal protection group or who falls off a truck and is taken home by a compassionate passerby, there is no fourth option.

A slaughterhouse is organized around a conveyer belt. Pigs and cows are unloaded from trucks into a pen. From the pen, they are herded single file onto a narrow fenced walkway called a chute, which leads into the slaughterhouse. In the chute, they can hear the screams of the animals ahead of them and smell the blood. They know what is about to happen to them, and often slaughterhouse workers have to strike them with lengths of pipe or shock them with electric prods (There's a reason they call them "cattle prods.") in order to force them through the gate to hell.

Other animals come off the trucks injured, sick, or too weak to walk. One slaughterhouse worker told humane investigator Gail Eisnitz how these "downers," as they are called, are treated:

> [Y]ou take a meat hook and hook it into his bunghole [anus]. You try to do this by clipping the hipbone. Then you drag him backwards. You're dragging these hogs alive, and a lot of the time the meat hook rips out of the bunghole. I've seen hams—thighs—completely ripped open. I've also seen intestines come out. If the hog collapses near the front of the chute, you shove the meat hook into his cheek and drag him forward.[24]

He is talking about animals who are conscious.

The chute leads to the stunning station, where the animals are shot in the head by a captive bolt gun or stunned with an electric shock and—it is hoped—knocked unconscious. After being stunned, the animal is shackled by a hind leg and hoisted to hang head down as she travels down the line, pulled along by an overhead conveyer. The problem is that the animals are unwilling to stand still so that they can be properly stunned, and management is unwilling to slow the line down to assure effective stunning. And so when the bolt hits off center, as it often does, or the stunner is unable to hold the electric gun against the animal long enough, the victims are shackled and hoisted while still conscious. Or, they may regain consciousness to find themselves hanging upside down by one leg, probably with an agonizingly dislocated hip or knee, with the stench of blood in their noses and the screams of other improperly stunned animals in their ears.

Another slaughterhouse worker told Eisnitz what happens to cows who are still conscious as they move down the line:

> Well, the leggers [employees whose job is to cut off the legs of the animals, NP] don't want to wait to start working on the cow until somebody gets down there to reknock it [stun the animal again; the leggers don't want to wait because that would slow down the line, get them in trouble, and possibly cost them their job, NP]. So they just cut off the bottom part of the leg with the clippers. When they do that, the cattle go wild, kicking in every direction.[25]

Imagine how it must feel to be dangling upside down, hanging by one leg, and then to watch somebody walk up with a giant pair of electric clippers and calmly cut your leg off. It is hard to know which would be worse, the pain, the horror, or the despair.

This employee told Gail Eisnitz that animals are sent along the line and carved up while they are still conscious "all the time."[26] Matthew Scully tells us that "The electrocuters, stabbers, and carvers who work on the floor wear earplugs to muffle the screaming" of the animals who are still conscious as they watch their own bodies being hacked into steaks and hams, pork chops, and hamburger.[27] But we Americans must have our meat. And so the line runs at the rate of 2,000 animals an hour.[28] Time is money, and who can afford to stop the line just to re-stun a conscious animal who won't live more than a few minutes, anyway?

The next time you eat a steak or a sausage link, take the moment that the slaughterhouse didn't, look at the piece of flesh on your plate, and ask yourself, "Did this come from an animal who watched himself being carved into pieces while he hung upside down on the slaughterhouse conveyer?" You won't have to ask that question at many meals before the odds make it a certainty that the answer has been yes at least once. After all, it happens "all the time."

. . .

Broiler chickens travel to slaughter in wooden or plastic battery cages, as many birds crammed into a cage as the "harvesters" can stuff in and still close the lid. The battery cages are stacked seven or eight high, front to back, side to side, on a flatbed 18-wheeler, an average of 5,000 chickens to a truckload.[29] Many times, I have seen these trucks plying the highways of the Delmarva Peninsula. Driving along behind one, your eyes are drawn to the chickens huddled in the cages, heads pulled down into their shoulders, bodies trembling. They are helpless; they are at the mercy of immensely powerful beings who show no mercy; they are doomed, and they know it. According to Karen Davis:

> The mass transportation of chickens is inherently cruel. As Compassion in World Farming states, as long as consumers demand the mass killing of chickens for food, these birds will "be manhandled, injured, covered in filth, hungry and thirsty, and just plain terrified from the moment they are caught [in the confinement shed, jammed into the battery cages, and loaded onto the

truck] to the time of their death at the slaughter-house."[30]

. . .

In the slaughter of mammals, there is at least an effort—no matter how inadequate—to render the animals unconscious. In the slaughter of birds, there is not even the effort. To make them controllable, chickens about to be slaughtered are first paralyzed by an electric shock. "Poultry slaughtered in the United States are neither stunned (rendered unconscious) nor anesthetized (rendered pain-free) . . . despite the use of the term "stun" to denote what is really immobilization by means of painful electric shocks."[31] Voltages high enough to cause unconsciousness are believed by slaughterhouse operators to cause capillary hemorrhaging, which renders the meat unfit to sell; no one wants a bloody Chicken McNugget.[32]

There are several methods of immobilizing poultry prior to slaughter, but the method favored by the giant slaughter-houses that supply most of the chickens to supermarkets and restaurants is called the "electrified brine-water bath."[33] Karen Davis describes it this way.

> After the birds have been manually jammed into a moveable metal rack that clamps them upside down by their feet . . . their heads and necks are dragged through a 12-foot brine-bath trough called a stun cabinet for approximately seven seconds . . . [electrical] currents shoot through [their bodies]. . . . The birds exit the stunner with arched necks, open, fixed eyes, tucked wings, extended, rigid legs, shuddering, turned up tail feathers, and varying amounts of defecation.[34]

Once paralyzed, the chickens, still clamped upside down by the feet, have their throats slit; they die from exsanguination, conscious until they bleed out.

Mindful Eating

A large segment of this book will be devoted to "Buddhist" defenses of meat-eating. As you read them, hold in your mind the death and suffering described in these two chapters. And ask yourself, In the face of all of this innocent suffering, does it really matter whether the Buddha ate pork or permitted his disciples to eat meat that was "pure in three ways?" Does it really matter whether veganism is a form of attachment or animals kill each other in the wild? Does anything, in fact, matter except the suffering and death that we visit upon these billions of sentient beings every year?

There can only be one Buddhist response to this gratuitous, egregious cruelty. As you read this book, as you sit down to dinner, as you put on your leather shoes, never forget the lives and deaths of the animals. And do not hide from your own responsibility. The beginning of mindful eating is the realization that *eating meat is not about the meat-eater; it is about the animals who are tormented and killed.*

CHAPTER 3

MOTHER BEINGS

The animals whom we kill so cavalierly and on whom we inflict such suffering are sentient beings. In Buddhist scriptures this is taken for granted. It never occurred to the Buddha or his early followers that anyone might try to dispute it. And to this day, without significant exception, all Buddhist lineages teach that animals are capable of suffering and joy just as we are.

In reaching this conclusion, Buddhism is simply following common sense. Allowing for physiological differences, animals behave very much as we would in similar circumstances. When harassed or attacked, they either cringe and flee or bristle and charge. When injured they cry out or try to flee the source of the pain. Within the boundaries of their physiology, animals express emotions like fear, grief, anger, happiness, pleasure, and love with behaviors that are as easily recognized as the smiles, frowns, tears, and laughter of humans. Dogs smile by wagging their tails, cats by holding theirs erect, perhaps with a little curl at the top like a shepherd's crook. Chimpanzees show fear by baring their teeth in an expression that resembles a human smile, a trait that has misled generations of movie and nightclub patrons into thinking that performing chimpanzees were happy when in fact they were terrified. Skunks show fear by lowering their heads and patting their front feet on the ground; anyone who does not back away quickly will soon wish she had. The point is, while the expressions of emotion are in some degree specific to the species, the emotions that they reveal are the common property of sentient beings.

Cognitive ethologist Marc Bekoff of the University of Colorado quotes with approval Rick Bass, an eco-Buddhist outdoor writer and novelist, who told an interviewer, "I think we can know how they [animals, NP] are feeling. . . . Anyone who's been around animals knows that. . . . It's madness to set up this artificial—for whatever perverted reason—this artificial barrier between humans and animals, saying that one has no contact or ability to tell what the other one feels or what moods there are between species. It's the craziest thing I have ever heard of."[1]

Physiologically, the more complex animals have the same five senses that we do—and in some instances one or two more. Migratory birds, for instance, can perceive, and navigate by, the earth's magnetic field. The complex animals have nervous systems—whether centralized, as in the case of vertebrates; or decentralized as with some crustaceans, such as lobsters and shrimp—that are fully capable of processing and transmitting sensations. And all vertebrates have brains that are highly developed in the areas that process both physical and emotional sensations. Nonhuman animals have the physical equipment to support pleasure and pain, joy and suffering. Some of the less complex animals may have fewer senses than we, but they do have senses. And while their nervous systems and brains may be less developed than ours, they are able to act intentionally, and therefore, they are—as the Buddha told us 2,500 years ago—conscious.

The Crab and the Earthworm

Presumably, as we go down the ladder of complexity, the complexity of the emotions diminishes proportionately. I have no way of knowing whether crabs, let us say, or—to drop down considerably farther—earthworms can experience grief, love, or jealousy. Dogs, cats, cows, pigs, geese, and parrots certainly can, and I have every reason to believe that other equally complex animals can as well. But about crabs, earthworms and the like, I do not know. What I do know is that as the complexity of the being declines, the most basic, most urgent emotions are the last to disappear from our view. Perhaps this is because the more complex emotions themselves cease to exist, or it may be because the less complex beings have no way within the limits of their physiology and our opportunities to observe them to express those emotions in ways that we can recognize.

I am ashamed to say that when I was a child, long before I knew better, I liked to go crabbing in a salt-water creek near my grandfather's farm. I would lure the crabs to the surface with a morsel of fish tied to a piece of string and dip them out of the water with a long-handled net. Then I would carry the crabs home in a bushel basket, where my aunt would dump them into a stew pot half-filled with water and seasoning, lift the pot onto the stove, and turn on the heat. As the water began to warm, you could hear a rustling noise start up in the stew pot like a breeze blowing through dry autumn leaves. As the water grew hotter, the rustling grew louder and quicker until it reached the crescendo of a storm. If I stood on tiptoe and lifted the lid of the pot, I could see the crabs scrambling for their lives, struggling desperately to climb up the slick, enameled sides of the pot. They were being scalded alive; they were in agony; and they were terrified. They were trying to escape, just as you or I would if we were facing death in that stew pot. Then gradually the rustling subsided, as one by one the doomed creatures succumbed to the boiling water and sank lifeless to the bottom.

During a rainstorm, earthworms come up out of their tunnels to avoid drowning. Searching blindly for safety, they sometimes crawl onto the sidewalk and lack the strength to get across. Stranded, deprived of nourishment, and either waterlogged and drowning or dehydrated and burned by the sun, they writhe helplessly, struggling for their lives until the last of their strength is gone. They resemble nothing so much as a human being who has fallen into the ocean and flails desperately to keep afloat until he is too exhausted to struggle any longer.

There is much we do not yet understand about the interior lives of animals, much less animals who are very different from us and whom we have little opportunity to observe in their natural setting. But this much is clear. The more complex animals have rich emotional lives, not at all dissimilar to ours. And in even the less complex animals, hatred of pain and love of life are as powerful as they are in us. If my pain is evil to me, the crab's pain is just as evil to the crab. If my life is dear to me, the earthworm's life is just as dear to the earthworm. At the most profound and urgent level, the crab, the earthworm, and I are brothers and sisters. And our membership in the family of sentient beings is the basis for the empathy that leads us to compassion for all living beings.

. . .

The sentience of animals, even the less complex animals, should not be surprising. Fear and desire, pain and pleasure at levels of intensity too acute to be ignored serve vital evolutionary functions. They preserve the individual and propagate the species. It would be astounding if they suddenly appeared on the tree of evolution at the point at which humanity first branched off. In fact, it seems obvious that had they not appeared far lower on the tree—and far deeper in the past than our species extends—evolution would never have progressed far enough to produce us.

Sentience would seem to be essential to any being who survives and reproduces by discretionary activity. Without sentience, including emotional sentience, a being would have no reason to choose one type of behavior over another and no motivation to survive and reproduce. If these behaviors were merely the result of complex programming, as some have claimed, there is no evolutionary reason why programming should have been replaced by sentience when we appeared on the scene. Discontinuities of this magnitude simply do not appear in the evolutionary record. Conversely, sentience has no survival or reproductive value for plants, and therefore, in the absence of evidence to the contrary, we may presume that they do not possess it.

· · ·

It should also come as no surprise that the most basic and most intense sensations—pain, pleasure, fear—should appear the earliest and be found in the more ancient and less complex forms of animal life. These basic sensations at a high level of urgency would be essential to survival and reproduction, whereas the more complex and subtle emotions, such as love, jealousy, gratitude, and anger, would appear later on the scene in beings whose survival and propagation depend on nuanced relationships with other sentient beings.

Supporting this idea, Marc Bekoff cites a study by Dr. Michel Cabanac of the Department of anatomy and physiology of Laval University in Quebec, which indicates that "the first mental event to emerge into consciousness was the ability of an individual to experience the sensations of pleasure or displeasure."[2] Cabanac believes that this event occurred between the appearance of amphibians and reptiles. That is, he believes that reptiles have this ability, while amphibians and fish do not.[3] What seems far more likely, however, is that amphibians and fish, since they survive and reproduce by discretionary activity, do experience pain and pleasure but do not evidence it in ways that Dr. Cabanac's methodology was able to detect.

Using a more sophisticated methodology, Dr. Lynne Sneddon of the School of Biological Sciences of the University of Liverpool recently directed a study of piscine pain conducted by a team of scientists from the prestigious Roslin Institute and the University of Edinburgh. According to Dr. Sneddin, "To demonstrate pain perception it was necessary to prove that the fish's behavior was adversely affected by a potentially painful experience and that the behavioral change was not a simple biological reflex. Our research conclusively demonstrated evidence of pain perception."[4]

At some point as we descend the scale of complexity, we probably reach a place where the physiological mechanism is no longer adequate to support consciousness, and animals become like plants, capable of reflexive responses to stimuli, but not sentient. Precisely where this line between sentient and insentient beings should be drawn, I do not know. Worms and insects are certainly above it. Microorganisms are probably below it. But wherever scientific investigation ultimately places it, the line is certainly far lower than most of us have been willing to consider.

The Homeless Dog and the Dalai Lama

For reasons not at all related to our subject, Buddhism does not employ the term "soul."[5] In order not to create the false impression that what is beyond human understanding can, in fact, be described, Theravadin teachers typically refrain from giving any name at all to whatever it is that is conscious, journeys through samsara, and is able to attain nirvana. Mahayana teachers often refer to this indefinable something as "Buddha nature," "true nature of mind," or "the clear light of awareness," terms that point to it without trying to define it. It is a teaching fundamental to both schools that *the Buddha nature of every living being without exception is identical.* (For convenience, I will use the Mahayana term.) As my teacher, Lama Kalsang Gyaltsen, once told me, "There is no difference between the Buddha nature of His Holiness the Dalai Lama and the Buddha nature of the most unfortunate homeless dog on the street."[6] Thus, at the most profound and important level, Buddhism recognizes no hierarchy of sentient beings; all are equal, and all are equally capable, over the course of many lifetimes, of gaining enlightenment. In fact, on our journey toward enlightenment, we will all experience many births as a mammal, insect, fish, etc., as well as human births.

On this foundation, Buddhism builds its teaching that all sentient beings—including land animals, birds, fish, cetaceans, reptiles, amphibians, crustaceans, insects, worms, all animals with the physical apparatus to support consciousness—are entitled to the protection of our compassion. First and foremost, *they are entitled to our compassion because they need it.* No further or more sophisticated reason is called for. Because animals share with us the ability to experience pleasure and pain, joy and sorrow, we can empathize with them, and out of that empathy arises the compassionate desire to free them from suffering and the loving desire to give them happiness. As the Buddha said, "All beings tremble before danger, all fear death. When a man considers this, he does not kill or cause to kill. All beings fear before danger, life is dear to all. When a man considers this, he does not kill or cause to kill."[7] Animals can suffer; therefore, we have a moral obligation to protect them from suffering in every way we can.

. . .

There are two other reasons why Buddhism instructs us to make all living beings equally the objects of our compassion. First, before we can attain nirvana, our compassion must encompass all who suffer. For both the Theravada and the Mahayana, enlightenment is a state of egolessness that can be attained only by those who have achieved *maha-karuna*, the great compassion that extends to all living beings without exception.

Second, all schools of Buddhism teach that reincarnation and transmigration are to be understood literally, as a real process. Mahathera Narada is quite explicit on this point, and no Eastern teacher that I am aware of would disagree with him. "Rebirth, which Buddhists do not regard as a mere theory, but as a fact verifiable by evidence, forms a fundamental tenet of Buddhism. . . ."[8] Some Westerners deny the validity of rebirth as part of an attempt to reconcile the Buddha's teaching to the contemporary Western worldview that they are unwilling to let go of. But, as the eminent Buddhist scholar Damien Keown of the University of London says, "Rebirth is one of the 'givens' of Buddhist thought and since its truth is universally assumed it is rarely asserted or defended as a dogma. . . . Some contemporary Buddhists have suggested that belief in rebirth is not an essential part of Buddhist teachings, but the notion is deeply engrained in the tradition and the ancient texts."[9]

In a similar fashion, some members of an earlier generation of Western Buddhists tried to interpret the teaching that human beings could be reborn as animals metaphorically, with different kinds of animals representing different kinds of unfortunate human circumstances. Saying that someone would be reborn as a pig meant that she would be reborn in squalor, and so forth. This was a speciesist misunderstanding of the dharma based on old Western habits of thought. Many in this first generation of Western Buddhists simply could not bring themselves to accept that there is no fundamental difference between human and nonhuman animals. Geshe Rabten, a Tibetan teacher who was extremely popular in the West, was unequivocal in disabusing his Western students of this view. "We may think that animals are a separate category of beings from us, that we cannot be reborn in such a state: this is a mistake. They are beings like us, reborn as animals because of certain actions they committed. If we accumulate that sort of karma, we too are sure to take animal rebirth."[10]

This passage by Geshe Rabten expresses the heart of the Buddhist teaching about animals. "*We may think that animals are a separate category of beings from us. . . . This is a mistake. They are beings like us. . . .*" Buddhism recognizes no essential distinction between humans and animals. There is no line that can be drawn between us, no Great Divide: *They are beings like us.* This is a point that I have made before and will make again because it is at once the doctrine that forms the foundation of Buddhist teaching about animals and a teaching that many Westerners find hard to accept.

Since, as Geshe Rabten tells us, a person who was a human in one life may be an animal in the next, and vice versa, the pig who was slaughtered to make the sausage you ate for breakfast this morning may, in a previous life, have been your grandfather. The battery hen who suffered a short, joyless life of unremitting pain while laying the eggs that accompanied your sausage may have been your mother. You yourself may be a veal calf in your next life.

A popular Buddhist technique for generating compassion is built on the idea that each of us has been travelling through samsara seeking enlightenment since beginningless time. Our journeys have taken so long, in fact, that at one time or another every sentient being in the universe has been our mother, who gave us life and showed us only kindness. Tibetan Buddhists often refer to all living beings, including animals, as "mother beings," to indicate that we are to hold them all as dear as we hold our own mothers, because at one time they were our mother. When we get up from the cushion, we should not leave this thought behind. Rather, we should keep it with us and hold it in our minds as we choose our food. That is the essence of eating mindfully.

There is a bit of Tibetan humor that tells of a lama who, because of his high level of realization, was able to see the past lives of the beings whom he encountered. Returning to his monastery after a solitary meditation retreat, he stopped at the home of a farmer for lunch. Back at the monastery the next day, he described the scene to his abbot. "The wife was cooking a fish, the husband and the eldest son were butchering a yak, and the daughter was swatting flies. In past lives, the fish had been the wife's sister, the yak had been the husband's father, and one of the flies had been their child. So the wife was frying her sister, the husband was slitting his father's throat and the son his grandfather's, while the daughter was squishing her baby brother. I couldn't stand it. I excused myself and went on my way. It was better to travel hungry than eat with those barbarians."[11]

CHAPTER 4

REASON AND RIGHTS

I n contrast to Buddhist teachers, Western philosophers
and theologians have not generally thought of animals as
"beings like us." Peter Harvey observes that "Rather than
divide the world into the realms of the 'human' and 'nature'
[as Western thought generally does], the classical Buddhist
perspective has seen a more appropriate division as that
between sentient beings, of which humans are only one type,
and the non-sentient environment . . ."[1] Buddhist teachings
express this division by referring to "the container"—the environment, comprising both our natural surroundings and
those that are human-made—and "the contents"—sentient
beings, both human and nonhuman. Buddhism groups animals with human beings. Western thought has tended to lump
them in with trees and rocks.

Waltzing on the Head of a Pin
In order to maintain the ethical separation of human from animal, Western thinkers have either had to deny that animals

are sentient or find some attribute other than sentience by which to grant entitlement to ethical treatment. The French philosopher Rene Descartes (1596–1650) denied that animals are sentient. In his *Discourse on Method*, published in 1634, Descartes called animals "automatons" and compared their cries of pain to the squeaking of a rusty hinge. In the early stages of the scientific revolution and continuing well into the nineteenth century, his views were influential in promoting the practice of vivisection. But they have long been discredited and no reputable scientist would any longer deny animals sentience.[2]

A more common approach to maintaining the great divide between human and animal was pioneered by Aristotle, who created a hierarchy in which moral status was determined by rationality, i.e. the ability to engage in the kind of abstract thinking that is reflected in questions like What is the meaning of life? or What is gravity? At the top of Aristotle's hierarchy were upper-class Greek men, and ranged below them—because they were allegedly less rational—were Greek tradesmen, women, slaves, barbarians (everyone who didn't speak Greek), and, lowest of all, animals, who Aristotle believed were capable of practical problem solving—finding food, escaping from danger, and similar activities—but were totally incapable of abstract thought. In Aristotle's hierarchy, the "lower" existed to serve the "higher," and all duties flowed upward. Women existed to serve men, slaves to serve free men, tradesmen to serve aristocrats, and so on. Animals, being at the bottom of the chain, existed solely to serve human beings and had no claim to ethical consideration.

In the Middle Ages, Saint Thomas Aquinas, the premier philosopher of the Catholic church, played a Christian riff on Aristotle's theme and declared that since only human beings have "rational souls," we have ethical duties only to other human beings. This notion of a qualitative difference between humans and animals based on reason, intelligence, or some other mental capacity, such as tool-making or the use of language, has dominated Western thinking about animals ever since, and has been widely used to justify our exploitation and abuse of them.

Can They Suffer?

Grounded exclusively in lovingkindness and compassion, Buddhist ethics protect all who need protection, which is to say, all beings able to suffer, regardless of their rationality, intelligence, use of language and tools, self-awareness, or any other extraneous factor. Buddhism has recognized from its inception what Enlightenment philosopher Jeremy Bentham said in 1789. "What else is it that should trace the insuperable line [between beings who are entitled to ethical treatment and those who are not]? Is it the faculty of reason, or perhaps the faculty of discourse? But a full-grown horse or dog is beyond comparison a more rational, as well as a more conversable animal, than an infant of a day, a week, or even a month old. But suppose the case were otherwise, what would it avail? The question is not, Can they *reason?* nor Can they *talk?* but Can they *suffer?*"[3]

As with Bentham, so with Buddhism. In an ethic based on compassion, there is only one relevant question, "Can they suffer?" Issues of reason, language, and the like are beside the point. If animals can suffer, it is wrong to inflict suffering on them. So far, so good. But at this juncture, Buddhism goes Bentham one better. Elsewhere in the same passage, Bentham says, "If the being eaten were all, there is very good reason why we should be suffered to eat such of them as we like to eat: we are the better for it, and they are never the worse. They have none of those long-protracted anticipations of future misery which we have."[4] In Bentham's view, animals have an interest in not suffering because they can suffer, but they have no interest in not dying because they cannot conceive of themselves as discrete, continuous beings whose lives extend into the future. Therefore, it is not wrong to kill animals for human benefit; it is only wrong to make them suffer in the process.

Philosophers in Denial

A star-studded array of philosophers and theologians has embroidered this lapse in Bentham's empathy into a full-blown defense of animal welfare and a rebuttal to animal rights. It has, in fact, become one of the dominant themes in the contemporary dialogue about animals and ethics. Popular Anglican theologian C. S. Lewis tells us that we must "distinguish between sentience and consciousness."[5] After warning us that this distinction "has great authority" and we would be "ill advised to dismiss it out of hand,"[6] he proceeds to describe sentience without consciousness as the awareness of individual, immediate sensations without any awareness that one sensation may be following another in succession. To put it in plainer language, a being that is sentient but not conscious would be aware of a sensation at the moment it was occurring, but would have no memory of past sensations, no anticipation of future sensations, and no sense of itself as a continuing being experiencing those sensations but separate from them. "If you give such a creature two blows with a whip, there are, indeed, two pains, but there is no co-ordinating self which can recognize that 'I have had two pains.' Even in the single pain, there is no self to say 'I am in pain'—for if it could distinguish itself from the sensation—the bed from the stream—sufficiently to say 'I am in pain,' it would also be able to connect the two sensations as *its* experience."[7] While he allows that this may not apply to "the apes, the elephants, and the higher domestic animals,"[8] (to any animal about whom Lewis has sufficient information that he can no longer deny the obvious?), he comforts himself with the vacuous speculation that "a great deal of what appears to be animal suffering may not be suffering in any real sense."[9]

This is—not to put too fine a point on it—sheer blather, and dismissal out of hand is exactly the treatment it deserves. Anyone who has had extended contact with animals knows that they have a sense of a continuing self. Animals recognize loved ones whom they have not seen for years, they impatiently await the dinner hour, and dogs often stand watch at the door when it is time for their human companions to come home from work. Animals who have been beaten with a stick will cower and cringe whenever someone picks up a stick, clearly anticipating future pain on the basis of remembered experience. This would not be possible if they did not possess the sense of themselves as discrete, continuing individuals. A being cannot avoid pain and seek pleasure, flee death and cling to life if she does not have a sense of herself as a discrete, continuing being. To speak of "sentience without consciousness" in any being capable of acting deliberately in his own self-interest is nonsense.

A refinement of this strange notion that animals lack a conscious self has appeared in the Vatican's semi-official newspaper, *L'Osservatore Romano*, under the byline of Marie Hendrickx, an influential theologian in the Office for the Doctrine of the Faith. "To have (at least virtually) the ability to perceive oneself and to act as an 'I' to a 'you' is specific to human beings."[10] Has Dr. Hendrickx never come home after a hard day at the Vatican to be greeted by her dog happily wagging his tail and affectionately nuzzling her hand? Has her cat never snuggled into her lap and begun purring with content-

ment? It is precisely their ability "to act as an 'I' to a 'you' "
that makes animals the beloved companions of so many people around the world.[11]

Even Peter Singer, the Australian ethicist whose 1975 book
Animal Liberation jump-started the modern animal rights
movement, is not immune. "When I say that all animals—all
sentient creatures—are equal, I mean that they are entitled to
equal consideration of their interests, whatever those interests
may be. . . . When it comes to the wrongness of taking life, for
example, I've always said that different capacities are relevant
to the wrongness of killing."[12] Singer's first statement, like
Freud's notorious dictum that "Anatomy is destiny," contains
a germ of truth but does not support the argument in his second statement. The truth in Freud's claim is that men are destined never to give birth and women never to impregnate
anyone, not that men are suited for power and mastery and
women for subservience and submission. Likewise, Singer's
statement means that you and I have an interest in the right to
vote and drive a car, whereas our companion animals do not;
their "capacities" render those rights meaningless for them.
But our companions—and with them all sentient beings—
have every bit as vital an interest in not being killed as we do.

The Buddha agreed with Singer that all sentient beings are
entitled to equal consideration of their interests, but he and
Singer part company on the wrongness of killing being related
to capacities. Buddhist scriptures always use the term "sentient beings" or "living beings" without qualification. There is
never a hint in Buddhist teachings that intellectual ability, a
sophisticated sense of self, or any characteristic beyond the
ability to suffer is relevant to moral standing. And this egali-
tarian approach to ethics acknowledges a fundamental truth
that is often ignored or denied in the West. *For ethical purposes, sentience is an absolute; either you have it—like humans*

and animals—or you don't—like plants and rocks. The complexity of the brain and the levels of intellectualization that a being is capable of (his "capacities" as Singer calls them) are not germane to the question of whether he is entitled to ethical treatment.

Supposedly objective standards of suffering are irrelevant because they are meaningless. Suffering is not an objective phenomenon; it is entirely subjective and can only be judged by the degree of distress that it inflicts on its subject. *The suffering of crabs and earthworms is as urgent to them as my suffering is to me, and for that reason, their suffering carries the same moral weight as my own.* The chicken and the fish have the same right to life and to freedom from fear and pain that I do because they have the same aversion to suffering and death that I have. Indeed, if I am a devout Buddhist, they have a greater dread of death than I have, because I have some inkling of what is to come, while they are very likely staring into a great dark abyss.

CHAPTER 5

THE GREAT COMPASSION

Buddhism—like its sister Indian religions, Hinduism and Jainism—is a way of liberation. It teaches that we are trapped by our negative emotions—greed, anger, hatred, fear, desire, and the like—in an illusory world of suffering that has much in common with a nightmare. Just as there is no escape from a nightmare except to awaken to the higher level of consciousness that is wakefulness, there is no escape from samsara, as this world of pain is called, except to awaken to the higher level of consciousness known as nirvana. This awakening, called enlightenment, is the goal of Buddhist practice. For until we achieve enlightenment and attain nirvana, we will be born in pain, live in pain, and die in pain. Not even death will bring relief, because it is the nature of living beings to be reborn again and again and again. We are being endlessly recycled through samsara because we are immortal and there is nowhere else to go except nirvana.

We break the cycle of rebirth and attain the eternal bliss of nirvana by gaining direct, intuitive insight into the true nature of the reality that lies hidden behind the illusions of samsara. This direct, intuitive experience is the only knowledge of that reality that is possible, because, being infinite and unitary, it is beyond the scope of conceptual thought and human language, both of which work by discrimination and analysis. Therefore, the true nature of the illusory sensory phenomena that form the world in which we live day to day is often called "emptiness" to indicate that the higher reality that lies hidden behind these phenomena is "empty" of—cannot be defined by—any of the concepts we use to understand and explain our everyday world. In Buddhist teachings, the immediate, non-conceptual insight by which we experience this higher reality "is the highest wisdom, which sees the Ultimate Reality."[1] And, in fact, "wisdom" is what it is usually called.

From an ethical standpoint, the Buddhist teachings on wisdom are important because they reveal the underlying unity of all existence. In some profound way that our intellects—which exist to organize and manipulate the illusory world that we must live in day to day—are not capable of comprehending, all being is one. This insight has radical implications for our treatment of the natural world. First, it means that the hierarchy so beloved of Western philosophers and theologians—"the great chain of being," as it is often called—has no place in the Buddhist understanding of the world. Everything that we see, hear, touch, taste, or smell is an epiphany—even though a garbled epiphany—of Ultimate Reality and Ultimate Truth. Therefore everything that we encounter in our daily lives is sacred, able to help us become aware of the Real and the True and arouse in us the sense of joy and awe that this awareness brings. This recognition of the potential in everything to introduce us to the sacred is what underlies Buddhist teachings on mindfulness. When we are truly mindful of our surroundings, not only is our awareness disciplined and focused, but it approaches the truth that undergirds the illusion.

We achieve wisdom by the practice of spiritual disciplines such as meditation, mindfulness, and chanting. The specific techniques vary from school to school. But for any of these training regimes to be effective, we must first have prepared our minds by developing compassion. Just as no amount of training will lead to peak performance for an athlete who gets drunk every night and gorges on junk food, no amount of meditation will generate wisdom in a mind that harbors enmity or indifference toward others. Hostility and callousness divide, and we cannot live in the awareness of the unity of all being while we insist on our own separateness.

May All Beings Be Happy

Buddhist compassion includes two elements. The first, usually called "lovingkindness," is the desire for beings to be happy. Bhante Henepola Gunaratana, a Theravadin monk from Sri Lanka and Abbot of the Bhavana Society monastery in West Virginia, describes Buddhist lovingkindness, for which he coins the term "loving-friendliness," as "a sense of interconnectedness with all beings. Because we wish for peace, happiness, and joy for ourselves, we know that all beings wish for these qualities. Loving-friendliness radiates to the whole world the wish that all beings enjoy a comfortable life with harmony, mutual appreciation, and appropriate abundance."[2]

The second element of Buddhist compassion is compassion narrowly defined. If lovingkindness is the desire for others to be happy, compassion in this stricter sense is the desire that they be free of suffering. Mahathera Narada equates compassion with *ahimsa*, nonviolence. "[Compassion] has the characteristic of a loving mother whose thoughts, words, and deeds always tend to relieve the distress of her sick child. It has the quality of not being able to tolerate the sufferings of others. Its manifestation is perfect non-violence and harmlessness—that is, a compassionate person always appears to be absolutely non-violent and harmless."[3]

A well-known Buddhist prayer expresses both aspects of Buddhist compassion.

> *May all beings be happy and have the cause of happiness.*
> *May they be free of suffering and the cause of suffering.*

. . .

Walpola Rahula tells us that, "According to Buddhism, for a man to be perfect, there are two qualities that he should develop equally: compassion (*karuna*) on the one side, and wisdom (*panna*) on the other."[4] Among the nine "Basic Points Unifying the Theravada and the Mahayana," that Bhante Rahula presented to the first convening of the World Buddhist Sangha Council in Sri Lanka in 1967, he included this: "Following the example of the Buddha, who is the embodiment of Great Compassion (*maha-karuna*) and Great Wisdom (*maha-prajna*), we consider that the purpose of life is to develop compassion for all living beings without discrimination and to work for their good, happiness, and peace; and to develop wisdom leading to the realization of Ultimate Truth."[5] A popular Buddhist saying has it that compassion and wisdom are like the two wings of a bird. Without both wings, the bird cannot fly; without compassion and wisdom, a person cannot attain nirvana. Most Buddhist teachings can be viewed as training manuals that teach various techniques, such as different forms of meditation, for generating compassion and wisdom.

In the Mahayana, this combination of infinite compassion

and wisdom is known by the Sanskrit word *bodhichitta,* "enlightened mind." Compassion is known as "relative bodhichitta" or "conventional bodhichitta" and wisdom is called "ultimate bodhichitta." The development of bodhichitta is the goal of all Mahayana practice. Those who have perfected it— known as *bodhisattvas,* "enlightened beings"—are so moved by compassion that they forego the bliss of nirvana and are voluntarily reborn in samsara for countless lifetimes to alleviate the suffering of those still trapped in the terrible cycle of birth and death.

First, Do No Harm

Earlier, I quoted Venerable Walpola Rahula, who told us that "Ethical conduct is built on the vast conception of universal love and compassion for all living beings, on which the Buddha's teaching is based."[6] *Buddhist ethics are expressions of lovingkindness and compassion,* nothing more, nothing less. They are at once a mental exercise program for developing boundless compassion for all living beings and guidelines for putting that compassion into practice in our daily lives. According to the Dalai Lama, "We can say that an act is immoral or improper to the extent that it causes harm to others."[7] That is to say, to the extent that it expresses a lack of compassion.

Our ability to feel compassion is based on our ability to feel empathy. Because I suffer, I know that other sentient beings suffer, and I know that they find suffering as repugnant as I do. Therefore, virtue resides first in not causing suffering and second in relieving it. The *Dhammapada,* a collection of the Buddha's sayings that forms part of the Pali Canon, is the most widely known and best-loved scripture in Buddhism. In it, the Buddha states this idea with unmistakable clarity.

All beings tremble before danger, all fear death. When a
man considers this, he does not kill or cause to kill.
All beings fear before danger, life is dear to all. When a
man considers this, he does not kill or cause to kill.

He who for the sake of happiness hurts others who
also want happiness, shall not hereafter find happiness.

He who for the sake of happiness does not hurt
others who also want happiness, shall hereafter find
happiness.[8]

This is the Buddhist counterpart to Jesus' saying that we
should do unto others as we would have them do unto us and
Hillel the Great's admonition not do to another what we
would not want done to us. It is also the classic Buddhist
statement of *ahimsa*, "not harming"—a doctrine which Buddhism shares with Hinduism and Jainism—according to
which our primary ethical obligation is not to harm other living beings. It is the same teaching that the Buddha gave to
Angulimala, the once and future Ahimsaka, *a true spiritual
practitioner does no deliberate harm.* Ahimsa is boundless, universal love and compassion put to work in the world.

The Five Commandments
Buddhism's specific ethical guidelines, its Ten Commandments, so to speak, which are common to all schools, are the
Five Precepts. These are: Do not kill, do not steal, do not lie,
do not commit sexual misconduct, and do not use intoxicants.
All are expressions of ahimsa. The first four prohibited actions
harm living beings directly, while the fifth attacks our judgment and self-control, paving the way for us to commit harmful acts and cause suffering to ourselves and others.

There are three things that it is important to note about the Five Precepts: First, the acts they prohibit are wrong because they cause suffering, not because a lawgiver, either divine or human, has said they are wrong. Therefore, in the strictest sense, they are not commandments at all, but instructions for applying ahimsa, the ultimate moral imperative, in our lives. Lying, for example, is wrong because it causes injury and destroys trust. Lies arise from greed, hostility, or fear; they are the enemies of lovingkindness. Even when it is not violent or coercive, sexual misconduct violates trust, breaks vows, and destroys families.

Second, although they are expressed in negative terms, the Precepts carry a positive meaning. Peter Harvey, Professor of Buddhist Studies at the University of Sunderland, observes that, "While each precept is expressed in negative wording, as an abstention, one who keeps them increasingly comes to express positive virtues as the roots of unwholesome action are weakened. Each precept thus has a positive counterpart. The counterpart of the first is [loving]kindness and compassion."[9] Tibetan Buddhist scholar, translator, and friend of the Dalai Lama Dr. Robert A. F. Thurman reminds us that "Not merely not killing, but *preserving* lives is the first of Buddhism's 'commandments.' "[10]

The Second Precept teaches us to be generous, while the Third instructs us to use our speech to benefit, heal, and bring together, not to exploit, injure, or divide. The Fourth Precept teaches that celibacy or a sexual relationship—whichever we choose—should be an expression of lovingkindness and compassion, not a manifestation of our ego. The Fifth teaches that we should put only wholesome nourishment into both our bodies and our minds.

Finally, since the Precepts are guidelines for practicing ahimsa, the First Precept, "Do not kill," is paramount and takes precedence over the others. Buddhism teaches, for example, that our speech should tend toward truthfulness and kindness; and when the two conflict, we should choose kindness.

Thou Shalt Not Kill . . . Anyone

Unlike the Biblical commandment, which Jewish and Christian authorities have typically applied only to human beings, the First Precept has always been held to apply to animals as well as humans. When discussing ethics and compassion, Buddhist scriptures and teachers refer to "living beings," or its synonym, "sentient beings," not "human beings." This usage is deliberate, and the terms are intended literally, applying the teachings to our treatment of all beings able to suffer, whether human or nonhuman. Both terms translate the same Sanskrit word, *prana* (Pali *pana*), which etymologically refers to anything that breathes. Since the ancient Indians, like other ancient peoples—including the Greeks and the Jews—identified the breath with the conscious vital essence of an individual, a breathing being was by definition a sentient being.

Within the Buddhist community, this has never been a matter of dispute; all schools agree on it. John Snelling, a well-known and highly respected Buddhist scholar and author, explains that "Taking life not only includes the murder of human beings, of course, but killing other living beings as well."[11] Peter Harvey is even more explicit. "The first precept, regarded as the most important, is the resolution not to kill or injure any human, animal, bird, fish, or insect."[12]

The Venerable Doctor Hammalawa Saddhatissa, a Sri Lankan monk who has also served on the faculties of several Western universities, emphasizes this aspect of the First Precept in a way that leaves no room for misunderstanding. "By the first precept, the Buddhist undertakes to abstain from destroying, causing to be destroyed, or sanctioning the destruction of a living being. *Living being* implies anything that has life, from insects up to and including man. In taking this precept, a Buddhist recognizes his relationship with all living things, a relationship so close that the harming of any living creature is inevitably the harming of himself. . . . The precept applies to all creatures irrespective of size. It does not exclude the killing of . . . lower animals."[13]

In the Mahayana tradition, Thich Nhat Hanh, the Vietnamese Zen monk who is among the most widely respected Buddhist teachers in the West, points out that, "In every country in the world, killing human beings is condemned. The Buddhist precept of non-killing extends even further, to include all living beings."[14]

Earning a Compassionate Dollar

The inclusion of animals under the protection of the First Precept is reflected in the Buddha's basic guidelines for a good and fruitful life, "The Noble Eightfold Path."[15] The fifth step on the Path is "right livelihood," which means earning a living in ways that are consistent with the five precepts and otherwise conducive to spiritual progress. Hammalawa Saddhatissa describes right livelihood as prescribing that "The layman should only pursue an occupation that does not cause harm or injustice to other beings. . . . The traditional trades from which the layman is barred are dealing in arms, in living beings, in flesh, in intoxicating drinks, and in poison."[16] Following that principle, in the world of today the list would include any occupation connected with: zoos, aquariums, and theme parks with animal attractions; animal acts in entertainment, including circuses, movies, rodeos, and nightclubs; hunting; fishing; whaling; the fur, leather, and silk trades; animal laboratories for biomedical research or product testing;

horse racing and dog racing; and, of course, bullfighting. In sum, any occupation that supports the killing of animals or infliction of suffering upon them is prohibited to Buddhists.

Thich Nhat Hanh makes a point concerning right livelihood that is of critical importance in our modern, commercial society: "[T]he butcher is not solely responsible for killing animals. He kills them for all of us who buy pieces of raw meat, cleanly wrapped and displayed at our local supermarket. The act of killing is a collective one. . . if we didn't eat meat, the butcher wouldn't kill it or would kill less. This is why right livelihood is a collective matter."[17] Kate Lawrence, a student of Nhat Hanh, takes her teacher's argument to its logical and inescapable conclusion: "[I]f these occupations [animal farmer, animal dealer, butcher] are clearly specified by the Buddha to be harmful, ought we to live in a way that requires other people to engage in these livelihoods? *If not, we cannot eat meat.*"[18] When we eat meat we are the reason that the butcher engages in a wrongful livelihood; we are as guilty as he is of violating the fifth step on the path.

By this same reasoning, we also cannot attend circuses with animal acts, rodeos, horse races, dog races, or bullfights. Nor can we visit zoos, aquariums, or theme parks that feature captive animals, or patronize animal acts in theaters and nightclubs. In order to live consistently with the requirement of right livelihood, we have to withhold our money and our applause from all who earn their living by animal exploitation.

The Peaceable Kingdom

From Magadha, where three centuries earlier the Buddha had lived and taught, the emperor Ashoka ruled a powerful empire that his grandfather, Chandragupta Maurya, had seized from a descendent of King Bimbisara, friend and patron of the Buddha. Thus, Ashoka was raised and educated in the place where

Buddhism's roots were deepest and strongest. Magadha was also a stronghold of Jainism, having been the home of Mahavira, and Chandragupta had been a Jain, as was Ashoka prior to his conversion to Buddhism.[19]

Returning from a triumphant campaign against a neighboring state, the conqueror was overwhelmed by the devastation, death, suffering, and sorrow that his war had caused. He resolved to devote the remainder of his reign to putting the Buddhadharma into practice as public policy. Renouncing all wars of aggression and conquest, Ashoka greatly reduced the size of his army and set about creating something unique in the history of the world: a profoundly compassionate state dedicated to relieving the suffering of all who lived within the orbit of its power.

When he became a Buddhist, Ashoka did not stop being a politician. In the best political style of the ancient world, he erected stone billboards all across his empire bragging about his achievements. But where other emperors bragged about the peoples they had conquered or exterminated and the great wealth and power they had amassed, Ashoka bragged of his charitable works and the good he had done for all who lived under his rule. These billboards, several of which have been found, catalogued, and translated, are known as "Pillar Edicts" if they are engraved on carved stone pillars and "Rock Edicts" if they are engraved in living rock. From our perspective, the most striking thing about the Edicts of Ashoka is their inclusion of animals under the protection of the government because Ashoka understood the Buddhadharma to require the protection of animals as well as humans.

In Pillar Edict 7, Ashoka tells us, "Along roads I have had banyan trees planted so that they can give shade to animals and men. . . . [A]nd in various places, I have had watering-places made for the use of animals and men."[20] "Everywhere has [Ashoka] made provision for two types of medical treatment: medical treatment for humans and medical treatment for animals..."[21] "To two-footed and four-footed beings, to birds and aquatic animals, I have given various things including the gift of life."[22]

By itself, this might not be so impressive were it not for other, more radical, edicts. "Here (in my domain) no living beings are to be slaughtered or offered in sacrifice."[23] And "Twenty-six years after my coronation various animals were declared to be protected." There follows a list of 24 species including parrots, geese, ducks, fish, turtles, pigeons, porcupines, squirrels, deer, and donkeys.[24]

It would appear that not everyone in Ashoka's empire was as dedicated to ahimsa as the monarch, whose efforts to create a state in which animals were protected encountered resistance. "The Dhamma regulations I have given are that various animals must be protected. And I have given many other Dhamma regulations also. But it is by persuasion that progress among the people through Dhamma has had a greater effect in respect of harmlessness to living beings and non-killing of living beings."[25] As he was committed to ruling with as little violence as possible, the techniques typically used by ancient despots to coerce obedience were not available to Ashoka, and so he had to employ what we would call public relations campaigns. In some cases, according to the edicts, he even found it necessary to compromise by limiting some of his reforms to certain periods of the month or specific holidays, and by not flatly banning the killing of all animals used for food.

Some of this resistance may have come from within the palace, because elsewhere he tells us that "Formerly, in the [royal] kitchen . . . hundreds of thousands of animals were killed every day to make curry. But now with the writing of this Dhamma edict only three creatures, two peacocks and a deer are killed, and the deer not always. And in time, not even these three creatures will be killed."[26] Ashoka viewed his compromises as temporary expedients until his public education campaigns could win the people over to nonviolence toward all living beings.

Ultimately he failed. Upon his death, Ashoka's heirs quickly undid his reforms, and to this day he remains the only historically important ruler in all of human history to come close to creating a state that protects and nurtures all who live at its mercy. Still, Ashoka was not without influence in the Buddhist world, especially in China, where several rulers in the seventh and eighth centuries emulated him by restricting hunting and meat-eating.[27]

As the ruler of the Mauryan Empire, Ashoka understood that the Buddhadharma called upon him to extend the protection of the state to all living beings, not just humans. In a democracy, the people rule. And the Buddhadharma calls upon us to insist that our elected officials likewise extend the protection of the state to all living beings. To be compassionate and just, a government must protect everyone who lives within its power, not just those who happen to be human.

CHAPTER 6

THUS HAVE I HEARD

A s we noted in the Introduction, Buddhism has two sets of scriptures: the Pali Canon, written in Pali, and the Mahayana scriptures, which were written in Sanskrit. In order to understand the controversy over the Buddha's attitude toward meat-eating, we will have to take a brief look at the development of these two scriptures and their relationship to one another.

As a scion of the wealthy and powerful kshatriya caste, which provided rulers, administrators, and military officers for ancient Indian society, the Buddha was well educated. He was literate, both in Sanskrit, the classical literary and religious language of India, and one or more dialects of Magadhi, the language of the region where he lived and taught in what is now northeastern India and southern Nepal. Since many of his followers were members of lower castes who could not speak Sanskrit, traditional sources and modern scholars agree that he taught in some form of Magadhi.

The Pali Canon

On several occasions, the Buddha specifically refused to appoint a successor, telling the monks that they should rely upon his teachings to guide them after his death. Therefore, three months after he passed into nirvana, 500 senior monks held a conference near the town of Rajagriha (Pali: Rajagaha; modern Rajgir), the capital of Magadha, where the Buddha had spent most of his life, to determine the future course of the movement. As the Buddha had written nothing down, the principal task of this First Buddhist Council was to reach agreement on an accurate text of his teachings. Several of the Buddha's closest followers, most notably Ananda, his cousin and personal attendant, recited the master's sermons to the assembly, which they then voted to accept as the authentic teachings of the Buddha. Each recitation began with the formula, "Thus have I heard," indicating a direct link to the Buddha, not mediated by hearsay. But another group of monks, also said to number 500—the number is not to be taken literally in either instance—dissented and declined to accept the Council's version of the Buddhadharma as authentic; they had their own version of the Buddha's teachings, although how it differed from the Council text we do not know.[1]

And so from the time of the Buddha's death, there has been no agreement on what constitutes the "original Buddhism taught by the Buddha." Lacking a central unifying authority, within a century or so Buddhism had split into several sects, each with its own scriptures—which certainly had a lot in common, but were not identical. Tradition holds that there were 18 of these early Buddhist denominations, but modern scholars believe the number was likely even higher.[2]

Further clouding the picture is the question of language. There is a saying in India that when you travel, you encounter a new language in every third village that you come to. In the

Buddha's day, things were no different. The unifying national language was Sanskrit, but it was spoken and understood only by the upper classes. In the northeastern region, where the Buddha lived and taught, ordinary folk spoke a number of closely related dialects derived from Sanskrit; these are usually grouped together under the name Magadhi.

One of the Magadhi dialects is called Ardhamagadhi, or "half-Magadhi," because it blends Magadhi with another nearby language. Ardhamagadhi is the language of Jain scriptures and is traditionally held to be the language of Vardamana Mahavira, who revitalized the ancient Jain religion. Since Mahavira and the Buddha were contemporaries living in the same area, it is sometimes thought that Ardhamagadhi was also the language of the Buddha. More likely, both the Buddha and Mahavira spoke several Magadhi dialects and taught in whichever one would be most easily understood by their listeners. This, I believe, is the origin of the legend that when the Buddha spoke everyone in his audience heard him speaking the listener's own language.

Even so, as Buddhism spread out from its birthplace, the scriptures, which still existed only in oral form, had to be translated into different languages. The Buddha himself is said to have approved this process, but to have forbidden the translation of his teachings into Sanskrit, apparently afraid that the elite language would drive out the popular dialects and make his teachings inaccessible to the common people.[3] Theravadin tradition holds that Pali is, in fact, the form of Magadhi that the Buddha spoke and that the Pali Canon contains his actual words. Modern scholars, however, believe that Pali is a later development, a standardized derivative of Magadhi deliberately created to be a *lingua franca* in which the Buddhist scriptures could be understood over a wide area.[4]

"All this," says John Snelling, "[when] added to the long

oral phase when changes must inevitably have crept in, means that we cannot say with certainty of anything that these are the precise words of the Buddha."[5] A half-century earlier, Heinrich Zimmer, perhaps the twentieth century's most influential Western Indologist, came to the same conclusion. "In the Buddhist texts there is no word that can be traced with unquestionable authority to Gautama Shakyamuni."[6] Edward Conze, the premier Western historian of Buddhism, is more emphatic:

> Of the actual words of the Buddha nothing is left. The Buddha may have taught in Ardhamagadhi, but none of his sayings is preserved in its original form. As for the earliest Canon, even its language is a matter of dispute. All we have are translations of what may have been the early Canon into other Indian languages, chiefly Pali and a particular form of Buddhist Sanskrit. . . . The original gospel is beyond our ken now. The farthest back we can get in time is the period when the community split up into separate sects.[7]

Some 200 years after the death of the Buddha, the Emperor Ashoka devoted himself to spreading the Buddhadharma throughout the Indian subcontinent. As part of this effort, he convened the Third Buddhist Council, which codified, still in oral form, the version of the Tripitaka that would become the direct ancestor of the Pali Canon. This is the earliest date that can reasonably be claimed for the existence of a standardized text of the Buddhist scriptures.

Next, Ashoka sent missionaries, including his own son and daughter, to distant Sri Lanka, where Buddhism quickly took hold. Three hundred years later (32–35 CE), a committee of monks met in a Sri Lankan cave in what Theravadins call the

Fourth Buddhist Council.[8] These monks reduced their version of the scriptures to writing, the first time, insofar as we know, that any Buddhist scripture had been written down. The result—five centuries after the Buddha's death—was the Pali Canon.

And so the claim that the Pali Canon contains the actual, original words of the Buddha cannot be sustained. The text of the Buddha's teachings was disputed within three months of his death and has been continuously disputed ever since. The Pali Canon, translated from earlier Magadhi dialects at some unknown time and place, and subject to deletions, elaborations, and editing over the 500 years that the Buddha's teachings existed only in oral form, records one of the early versions of the Buddhadharma, and it must be given great respect and authority. But it records by no means the only early version. Even if, as is sometimes claimed, it faithfully reproduces the version of the suttas recited at the First Buddhist Council (which, given the intervening centuries, is hardly likely), the Pali Canon cannot claim to be the *earliest* version of the Buddha's teachings, because a large number of Buddhist monks disputed the Council's text and found the issue serious enough to break from the larger group and transmit their own version of the Buddha's words. Whether the Pali Canon can claim to be the earliest version of the Buddha's teaching *still in existence* is a question that I will try to resolve when we consider the evolution of the Mahayana scriptures.

The Mahayana Sutras

The Mahayana scriptures were originally written in a simplified dialect known as "Buddhist Hybrid Sanskrit," which incorporates elements of regional languages like Magadhi and was probably developed to be intelligible to people whose classical Sanskrit was a little rusty. It may even be Sanskrit *as written by* people whose classical Sanskrit was a little rusty. Unfortunately, only portions of the Mahayana scriptures have survived into the modern era in the original language. A Chinese version known as the Chinese Tripitaka and a Tibetan version known as the *Kanjur* exist in more complete form, but the two are not identical. Thus, three versions of the Tripitaka still exist: a Theravadin edition in Pali, and two Mahayana editions, one in Chinese and one in Tibetan. To give you some idea of the scope of these works, in modern printed form the Pali Canon takes up about 50 volumes; the Chinese Tripitaka is slightly longer, and the Tibetan Kanjur nearly twice as long. We have to bear in mind that the Buddha taught for 45 years!

We do not know when the Sanskrit scriptures were first reduced to writing. They were translated into Chinese late in the fourth century CE, but according to Rupert Gethin, Director of the Centre for Buddhist Studies at the University of Bristol, "[T]he texts upon which they rest must like the Nikayas [the Pali Canon] date from the centuries before the Christian era."[9] In short, the teachings conveyed in the Mahayana sutras date from the same period as those contained in the Pali Canon. Some of the teachings in the Mahayana scriptures, especially those known as the "perfection of wisdom" teachings, clearly include later elaborations on earlier teachings. But there is no reason to automatically assume that every teaching in the Mahayana sutras that differs from Theravadin doctrine must be later in origin. Both sets of sutras contain material that originated with the Buddha and material that was added later.

"I Do Not Permit Meat-eating"
The Mahayana sutras portray the Buddha as issuing blanket, universal condemnations of meat-eating. Those who contend

that the Buddha permitted his followers to eat meat find no support in the Mahayana scriptures. The *Lankavatara Sutra*, in particular, devotes an entire chapter to the Buddha's response to the request of a disciple named Mahamati to "teach us as to the merit and vice of meat-eating"[10] "For innumerable reasons," the Buddha begins, "the Bodhisattva, whose nature is compassion, is not to eat any meat." (245)[11] He goes on to explain that every living being has at one time or another been our parent, sibling, child, or someone else who was very close to us. And it is entirely possible that they could be reborn in the present as an animal. "[This being so] how can the Bodhisattva-Mahasattva who desires to approach all living beings as if they were himself and to practice the Buddha-truths, eat the flesh of any living being that is of the same nature as himself?" (245)[12]

From that introduction, the Buddha proceeds to state the reasons why a Buddhist practitioner who is striving to gain enlightenment for the benefit of all living beings should abstain from meat. The primary reason is that meat-eating cannot coexist with the great compassion:

> Thus, Mahamati, wherever there is the evolution of living beings, let people cherish the thought of kinship with them, and thinking that all beings are [to be loved as if they were] an only child, let them refrain from eating meat. So with Bodhisattvas whose nature is compassion, [the eating of meat] is to be avoided by him. Even in exceptional cases, it is not [compassionate] of a Bodhisattva in good standing to eat meat. (246)[13]

But eating meat is not just spiritually unhealthy; it also damages your body and mind. After listing the physical and emotional ailments that are caused by eating meat—they range from loss of sleep and tremors to paranoia and intestinal parasites—the Buddha concludes:

> When I teach to regard food as if it were eating the flesh of one's own child, or taking a drug, how can I permit my disciples, Mahamati, to eat food consisting of flesh and blood, which is gratifying to the unwise but abhorred by the wise, which brings many evils and keeps away many merits; and which was not offered to the rishis and is altogether unsuitable? (249)[14]

The reference to taking a drug strongly suggests that the Buddha regarded meat-eating as a violation of the Fifth Precept as well as the First. Picking up on this theme, Thich Nhat Hanh and Kate Lawrence regard any kind of consumption that harms oneself or others (including animals) to be contrary to the spirit of the Fifth Precept. Lawrence specifically cites meat-eating, saying that " . . . meat qualifies as a toxic substance, and thus violates the practice of this precept."[15]

Meat-eating is also a source of negative karma that causes rebirth in realms of great suffering from which is it hard to gain release:

> In the life of transmigration, Mahamati, such ones [meat-eaters] will fall into the wombs of such excessive flesh-devouring creatures as the lion, tiger, panther, wolf, hyena, wildcat, jackal, etc.; they will fall into the wombs of still more greedily flesh-devouring and still more terrible Rakshasas. Falling into such, it will be with difficulty that they can ever obtain a human womb; how much more [difficult] attaining Nirvana! (252)[16]

Next the Buddha approaches the issue from a somewhat different angle—one that is especially relevant to the modern debate over meat-eating—by pointing out that the meat-eater is ultimately responsible for the slaughter of animals:

> If, Mahamati, meat is not eaten by anybody for any reason, there will be no destroyer of life. (252)[17]

Again, the Buddha returns to the point that meat-eating and the great compassion cannot coexist and then repeats his injunction in absolute terms:

> Thus, Mahamati, meat-eating I have not permitted to anyone, I do not permit, I will not permit. . . . That I have permitted the Shravakas as well as myself to partake of [meat-eating], Mahamati, has no foundation whatever. (255–256)[18]

Finally, the Buddha summarizes his objections to meat-eating in 24 numbered statements—today we would call them "bullets." They include:

> 11. Those evil-doers go to the most horrifying hell; meat-eaters are matured in the terrific hells such as Raurava, etc.[19]

Rebirth in Raurava, "the screaming hell," is portrayed in Buddhist literature as the result of drinking alcohol, again suggesting that the Buddha regarded meat-eating as a violation of the Fifth Precept.

> 12. There is no meat to be regarded as pure in three

ways: not premeditated, not asked for, and not impelled; therefore, refrain from eating meat.[20]

23. [Meat-eating] is forbidden by me everywhere and all the time for those who are abiding in compassion; [he who eats meat] will be born in the same place as the lion, tiger, wolf, etc.[21]

In the *Brahmajala Sutra*, the Buddha says:

Disciples of the Buddha, should you willingly and knowingly eat flesh, you defile yourself. . . Pray, let us not eat any flesh or meat whatsoever coming from living beings. Anyone who eats flesh is cutting himself off from the great seed of his own merciful and compassionate nature. . . . This is why all Bodhisattvas should abstain from eating the flesh of any and all sentient beings. Someone who eats flesh is defiled beyond measure.[22]

In yet another Mahayana scripture, the *Surangama Sutra*, the Buddha teaches that meat-eaters cannot attain Nirvana:

[H]uman beings who might become enlightened and attain Samadhi, because of eating meat, can only hope to attain the rank of a great Raksha and until the end of their enjoyment of it must sink into the never ceasing round of deaths and rebirths. They are not true disciples of the Buddha. If they kill sentient beings and eat the flesh, they will not be able to escape from this triple world.[23]

The Buddha goes on to emphasize that meat-eating cannot

coexist with the great compassion and calls for not just a vegetarian, but a vegan lifestyle.

How can a bhikkshu, who hopes to become a deliverer of others, himself be living on the flesh of other sentient beings? Pure and earnest bhikkshus, if they are earnest and sincere, will never wear clothing made of silk, nor wear boots made of leather, because it involves the taking of life. Neither will they indulge in eating milk or cheese because thereby they are depriving the young animals of that which rightly belongs to them.[24]

Finally, the Mahayana *Mahaparinirvana Sutra* (not to be confused with the Theravadin *Mahaparinibbana Sutta*, which I will discuss shortly) reports that Kasyapa, one of the Buddha's most senior followers, proposed a total abstention from meat. The Buddha replied:

Well said, well said! . . . From now on, I do not permit my sravaka disciples to take flesh.[25]

Wishing to be absolutely clear on what the new rule entailed, Kasyapa asked the Buddha what a monk should do if offered a plate of food that included meat. As Zen practitioner, Buddhist scholar, and president of the United Kingdom Anti-Vivisection Information Society (UKAVIS), Tony Page, observes, "The Buddha was unequivocal."

Use water, wash off the meat, then take it [eat the rest of the meal]. . . . If one sees that there is much meat, one must not accept such a meal. One must never take the meat itself. One who takes it infringes the rule. I

now set this rule of segregating one's own self from taking meat.[26]

In the next section, we shall see that the Pali Canon reports
the Buddha giving a somewhat different answer to the question of what monks should do when they are offered meat by
householders, an answer that many claim opens a door to
meat-eating. I am always amazed that so many Mahayana Buddhists, especially in the West, seem eager to accept the Pali
Canon over the Mahayana scriptures on this point and only
on this point. It is eloquent testimony to the truth of the Buddha's teaching on the fearsome power of craving.

An Animal Slaughtered for You

The scriptural defense of meat-eating rests on several passages
in the Pali Canon, all of which state that Buddhist monks are
forbidden to eat meat unless they are certain that the animal
was not killed for them. The most important of these is a story
in the *Jivaka Sutta* in which the Buddha's personal physician,
Jivaka, tells him of rumors to the effect that the Buddha eats
meat from animals whom people have slaughtered for the
express purpose of serving him the meat. The Buddha denies
this, and explains his position on meat this way: "Jivaka, I say
that there are three instances in which meat should not be
eaten, when it is seen, heard or suspected [that the living
being has been slaughtered for oneself]. I say that meat should
not be eaten in those three instances. I say that there are three
instances in which meat may be eaten: when it is not seen, not
heard, and not suspected [that the living being has been
slaughtered for oneself]. I say that meat may be eaten in these
three instances."[27]

The words that the translators have placed in brackets,
"that the living being has been slaughtered for oneself," do not

appear in the Pali text. They were added by the translators for the sake of clarity. Pali omits words or phrases that can be inferred from the context far more often than does English. The translators' interpolation, "that the living being has been slaughtered for oneself," reflects the traditional understanding of this passage since antiquity.

Tony Page is the author of a monumental exploration and analysis of Buddhist scriptures, both Theravadin and Mahayana, from an animal rights perspective. In it, Dr. Page rejects the traditional reading and argues that "Surely the idea is that meat is not to be eaten if it is seen, heard from others, or suspected by oneself *to be meat.*"[28] Page believes that the Buddha meant to excuse only the accidental eating of meat, which incurs no blame because it involves no intent.

There is no doubt, as Page argues, that his interpretation accords better with the Buddha's teachings on ahimsa than the traditional reading. We cannot rule it out. Still, I do not find Page's explanation entirely persuasive. Implied phases are common in the Pali Canon, and they are typically to be understood on the basis of what immediately precedes them, not by reference to the Buddha's entire body of teaching. What immediately precedes the sentence in dispute is Jivaka's question about meat from animals killed specially for the Buddha. The traditional reading is responsive to Jivaka's question in a way that Dr. Page's is not.

Roshi Philip Kapleau, one of the pioneers of American Buddhism and founding abbot of the Rochester Zen Center, was a leading proponent of Buddhist vegetarianism. In his classic *To Cherish All Life: A Buddhist Case for Becoming Vegetarian*, Kapleau argues that the Buddha did not actually speak these words and that his teaching on meat is more accurately captured in the *Lankavatara Sutra* and other Mahayana scriptures. Nevertheless, he accepts the traditional reading of this passage in the *Jivaka Sutta* as referring to meat killed specially for oneself.[29] With some reluctance, I have to agree.

. . .

Let's presume for the moment that the traditional interpretation is correct and that the teaching did, in fact, originate with the Buddha. What does it mean? First and foremost, it means that the Buddha was creating an extremely narrow exception to a broad general rule. Buddhist monks begging their daily meal might accept meat only if they had no reason to suspect that the meat came from an animal who had been slaughtered for them. The exception presumes the rule. *Do not eat meat.* If there were no such rule, there would be no need for the exception. In fact, the exception reinforces the rule, because the Buddha expressly says that in all other circumstances, "Meat should not be eaten."

The Buddha and his disciples did no work, carried no money, and purchased nothing, not even food. Once a day, in the morning, they fanned out through whatever town they were near, begging food from householders. Whatever each was given went into his alms bowl, and when their bowls were full they went back to wherever they were staying to eat their only meal of the day. This system worked because in ancient India there was a long tradition of spiritual seekers begging their sustenance, and giving them leftover food was considered a virtuous act that would generate positive karma.

The only other way a monk might be served meat was by being invited to dinner with his own family or the family of a sponsor of the sangha. In the north of ancient India, a semi-tropical country without refrigeration, meat could be kept for only very short periods of time. Therefore, it was a common practice for the wealthy to place an order with a butcher for an animal to be killed on the day they were planning a banquet or other important meal. Thus a householder who wanted to serve meat to the Buddha and a group of his monks would have invited them to come on a specific day and then ordered the animal(s) whose flesh was to be served to be slaughtered several hours in advance. And so, allowing for the different logistics of shopping, the ancient phrase "an animal slaughtered for you" is synonymous with the modern phrase "an animal purchased by you or for you." *This saying in the Pali Canon directly prohibits Buddhists from purchasing meat in a supermarket or restaurant or eating meat that someone else has purchased.*

That the almsbowl exemption in the *Jivaka Sutta* applies *only* to the almsbowl and not to meat served at dinner is made clear in a passage toward the end of the same sutta, which emphasizes both the Buddha's abhorrence for meat-eating and the reason for it. Meat served at dinner would have been slaughtered for all who attended the dinner, including the Buddha and his disciples. It would have been served in the hope of gaining merit—positive karma—by making an offering to the Buddha and the sangha.

If anyone slaughters a living being for the Tathagata [the Buddha] or his disciples, he lays up much demerit [negative karma] in five instances. When he says: 'Go and fetch that living being,' this is the first instance in which he lays up much demerit. When that living being experiences pain and grief on being led along with a neck-halter, this is the second instance in which he lays up much demerit. When he says: 'Go and slaughter that living being,' this is the third instance in which he lays up much demerit. When that living being experiences pain and grief on being slaughtered, this is the fourth instance in which he lays up much demerit. When he provides the Tathagata or his disciple with food that is not permissible, this is the fifth instance in which he lays up much demerit. Anyone who slaughters a living being for the Tathagata or his disciple lays up much demerit in these five instances.[30]

When we buy meat in a supermarket or restaurant, we are telling the owner of the slaughterhouse to "Go and slaughter that living being." The fact that our order is given after the killing is nothing more than a quirk in the logistics of our mass-market economy. Morally, it changes nothing. We are still responsible for the suffering and death of the animals because they are slaughtered for those who buy and eat the meat. If people did not buy and eat the meat, animals would not suffer on factory farms and die in slaughterhouses.

. . .

Despite centuries of overinterpretation in defense of meat-eating, the reason for the Pali Canon's rule against buying meat or eating meat bought for you is quite straightforward. In the case of monks begging their daily meal, the meat came from an animal who had been killed for a class of people to which the monks did not belong: the householder, his family, and their dinner guests. Had the monk not come begging, the animal would have been killed anyway, and the small scraps he was given would not lead to the slaughter of another animal to replace the meat given away. But in the case of being invited to dine in the home of a family member or sponsor, if the monks had not been willing to eat it, the animal would not have died; therefore, the Buddha forbade his monks to eat meat served to them in people's homes. It is in this tradition that Thich Nhat Hanh, following practices handed down by the ancient Chinese masters, instructs members of his robed Sangha, "If you are invited to a meal . . . do not sit at a table where there is wine or meat."[31]

In our modern market economy, there is no way to consume meat, eggs, or dairy without making ourselves complicit in the suffering and violent death of many innocent animals. The meat sold in supermarkets and restaurants comes from animals who are killed for all who will buy or eat it. Animals are slaughtered in anticipation that someone will buy the meat, and the person who buys the meat does so in anticipation that someone will eat it. If no one ate the meat, no one would buy it; and if no one bought the meat, no one would kill the animals. We have already seen that in the Lankavatara Sutra, the Buddha makes this very point. "If, Mahamati, meat is not eaten by anybody for any reason, there will be no destroyer of life." When we buy meat, or eat meat that someone else has bought, we become the engine that powers the terrible killing machine called the meat industry. We cannot claim innocence by delegating our dirty work to someone else and hiding behind the mask of anonymity.

When we buy meat in a supermarket or a restaurant, the owner will purchase more meat to replace what we have bought. And so even if we could tell ourselves—which I cannot—that we are not responsible for the death of the animals whose flesh we purchase, there is still no way for us to evade responsibility for the killing of the animals whose flesh will replace the meat that we bought. As Thich Nhat Hanh tells us, "When we buy something or consume something, we may be participating in an act of killing. [The first] precept reflects our determination not to kill, either directly or indirectly, and to prevent others from killing."[32]

Pulling a Tech
When I was a kid on the playground, every now and then someone would "pull a tech." "Pulling a tech" meant trying to gain an advantage by citing a technicality in the rules, such as

invoking the three-second rule in a pickup game of basketball being played in somebody's driveway with a hoop nailed up over the garage door. Modern Buddhists who use the *Jivaka Sutta* to defend meat-eating are "pulling a tech"; they are trying to evade the spirit of the Buddha's teachings on lovingkindness, compassion, and ahimsa by citing a provision that is no more relevant to the modern world than the three-second rule is to kids' driveway basketball.

In jurisprudence, pulling a tech is called "taking advantage of a loophole." But, as I said earlier, Buddhist ethics are not a legalistic system of rules and regulations that can be fulfilled by literal adherence to the details. Buddhist ethics are about intention. They are guidelines for putting lovingkindness, compassion, and nonviolence to work in our daily lives. They cannot be divorced from that larger purpose. Therefore, there are no technicalities and no loopholes in Buddhist ethics. We either fulfill the intent or we do not. In eating the flesh of murdered animals, there is neither lovingkindness, compassion, nor nonviolence—only callousness and disregard for the suffering and death of living beings, no matter how clever we may be at finding loopholes.

CHAPTER 7

THE LAST SUPPER

The Buddha was part of a religious revival that swept
India for 200 years beginning in the seventh century
BCE and changed the spiritual and cultural landscape
of the subcontinent forever. Known as the *shramana* or
"renouncer" movement, its leaders were ascetics who sought
spiritual fulfillment though meditation, physical and mental
discipline, and the renunciation of worldly pleasures. Out of
the shramana movement grew Buddhism, modern Jainism,
and Hinduism as represented in the Upanishads, the Bhagavad
Gita, Yoga, and Vedanta.

Shramanic spirituality was based on three principles: 1) The
pursuit of liberation from an otherwise endless cycle of birth
and death in an illusory world of suffering. 2) Renunciation of
the worldly life in favor of meditation and ascetic discipline.
And 3) Strict adherence to ahimsa, including a vegetarian diet,
based on a belief in the ultimate unity of all life and the ethical
preeminence of compassion for all living beings.

Although this eased over time—in part due to the influence of Buddhism and in part due to their widening popularity—in their inception the shramana traditions were rigidly ascetic. Believing that there was no way to gain liberation except by controlling the mind and no way to control the mind except by bludgeoning the flesh into submission, ascetics undertook disciplines such as surviving on just a few grains of rice a day, staring directly at the sun until their eyes were burned out, lying for hours on beds of sharp nails, and sitting in awkward postures without moving until their joints froze into place and they could not move.

When he left home to take up the spiritual quest, the Buddha studied with these ascetics and practiced their austerities. In fact, his mental discipline was so great that he excelled at them and attracted a circle of five followers who believed that he would surely gain liberation and wanted to be there when he did. The Buddha starved himself to the point that he later said he could poke his belly with his finger and feel his backbone. But as a result, he grew weak, his mind became cloudy, and he lost the ability to concentrate. Realizing that the body is the only vehicle we have in which to gain liberation, he abandoned strict ascetic discipline in favor of the "Middle Way," a moderate lifestyle that neither coddled the body nor brutalized it. When he began his return to health by eating a bowl of rice and milk given him by a local peasant girl, his five followers decided that their faith in him had been misplaced and they abandoned him.

After he gained enlightenment, they repented and became history's first Buddhists. But the initial reaction of these five ascetics illustrates a problem of perception that would plague the Buddha throughout his career. To appreciate the tension that the Buddha's rejection of asceticism and adoption of the Middle Way created between him and the larger shramana community, imagine the reaction from the evangelical Christian world if Jerry Falwell were to announce that a little drinking, gambling, and fornicating are okay so long as they are done in moderation.

To the shramana community, the Buddha's Middle Way approach to lifestyle left him vulnerable to charges of laxity in other areas as well, including his commitment to ahimsa. Thus, the Buddha was forced to begin taking his monks into retreat during the rainy season because of complaints that by walking about during the rains when the grasses were fragile and tiny insects and worms came to the surface, they were killing living beings.

The Five Righteous Rules

Within the Buddha's sangha, there always seems to have been a contingent of monks who wanted to take the stricter approach of the Jains and other shramana ascetics. Eventually, not even the Buddha was able to prevent this rift from bursting into open schism. The leading figure among the "conservatives" within the Sangha was the Buddha's charismatic young cousin, Devadatta. Although the Buddhist scriptures portray Devadatta as motivated solely by envy and ambition, we have to remember that here, as elsewhere, history was written by the victors, and however envious and ambitious Devadatta may or may not have been, the issue underlying his schism was the alleged laxity of the Buddha in maintaining strict ascetic discipline and ahimsa.

Devadatta called on the Buddha to institute what he called "five righteous rules" based on strict shramana discipline. These rules were:

1) Monks could live only in the forest, not in monasteries or encampments near towns. The shramana movement had been founded by hermit-monks who lived in the

forests, and many still considered the forest the only fit dwelling for a spiritual seeker.

2) Monks could eat only food they had begged; they could not accept invitations to dine in the homes of laypeople. Dining in the homes of wealthy sponsors looked too much like indulging in the worldly pleasures that monks were supposed to renounce.

3) Monks could wear only robes they had sewn together themselves from rags and discarded pieces of old cloth that they had collected; they could not accept robes donated by laypeople.

4) Monks could not sleep under a roof, even during the rainy season.

5) Monks could eat no meat whatsoever. If they found scraps of meat in their begging bowls, they could not eat them.

Faced with this challenge to his monastic rule, the Buddha responded that in regard to the first three, his monks could follow their own consciences. Any monk who wished to live only in the forest, eat only food that he had begged, and wear only robes that he had made from rags was at liberty to do so. On the last two "righteous rules," he was more adamant. All members of his sangha were required to spend the rainy season in retreat, sleeping within the walls—and under the roof—of the monastery. And monks would have to accept whatever they found in their begging bowls, including meat, provided that they had not seen, had not heard, and had no reason to suspect that the animal had been killed so that the meat could be given to them.

As the story has come down to us, Devadatta led 500 monks out of the Buddha's sangha to form his own community. But shortly thereafter, two of the Buddha's closest followers visited Devadatta's headquarters and persuaded all of the breakaway monks to return to the fold, ending the schism.[1]

. . .

This friction between the Buddha and the more rigid wing of the shramana movement—and the existence of a "conservative" and "liberal" wing within his own sangha—are the keys to understanding why we have two versions of the Buddha's attitude toward eating meat placed in an almsbowl. The alternative version of the Buddha's teachings that surfaced immediately following the First Buddhist Council undoubtedly reflected the dharma according to the conservative wing of the sangha. If we had their scriptures, they would certainly portray the Buddha as forbidding monks to eat even scraps of meat placed in their begging bowls. This is the ancient tradition—as ancient as the tradition that ultimately entered the Pali Canon—that eventually found its way into the Mahayana Sutras. On the subject of eating meat placed in the almsbowl, the Pali Canon reflects the dharma according to the liberal wing of the sangha.

Pro and Con

So which is authentic? The two versions have existed side by side from the most ancient times. And there is no third-party testimony, so to speak, that could resolve the conflict. But this much we do know:

Neither the Pali Canon nor the Mahayana sutras was reduced to writing for at least 500 years following the Buddha's death.

Both versions report traditions that date to the same

period, the three to four centuries before the Pali Canon was written down.

Whether or not the Buddha espoused it, the idea that monks should not eat scraps of meat that they might find in their almsbowls dates back to his lifetime and to his own inner circle.

On the historical record, there is no reason to believe that the teaching on meat-eating in the Pali Canon is more likely to be authentic than the teaching in the Mahayana scriptures.

There are four possibilities:

The Pali Canon is correct, and the Buddha prohibited meat-eating with the sole exception of scraps placed in the begging bowls of monks. If this is true, the absolute prohibition against meat-eating was added by later generations of monks who favored the strict interpretation of Devadatta that was more in line with the general approach of the shramana ascetics. This is the view traditionally advanced by Theravadin practitioners and by Western Buddhists of all schools who don't want to give up their meat habit.

The Mahayana sutras are correct, and the Buddha prohibited monks from eating scraps of meat that unwitting householders might place in their almsbowls. If this is true, the almsbowl exception was added by later generations of monks who wanted to be able to eat meat. This is the traditional Mahayana view and the view advanced by Roshi Philip Kapleau.[2]

Neither set of scriptures is correct, and the Buddha advocated a position in regard to meat placed in begging bowls that has not been preserved. This is extremely unlikely, since it is hard to imagine what that position would have been. Either you can eat it or you can't. There doesn't seem to be a third choice.

Both sets of scriptures are correct, and the Buddha took both positions but at different times. The Pali Canon records several instances of the Buddha changing his mind about a practical issue, including decisions to take the sangha into monastic retreat during the rainy season and to ordain women. The former was done in response to criticism from the broader shramana community, while in the latter instance we are told that Ananda had to argue with the Buddha quite insistently before he would relent and admit women to the robed sangha.

If this speculation is correct—and I believe it probably is— then at the time of Jivaka's question and Devadatta's challenge, the Buddha took the position reflected in the Pali Canon. Then, at some later point, perhaps as a gesture of conciliation to the schismatics when they returned to the fold, he relented and established a rule against eating even the bits of meat that were placed in begging bowls. But his sangha remained divided on this issue, and subsequently each group recorded only the teaching that its own practice followed and erased the other from memory. The Mahayana *Mahaparinirvana Sutra* would seem to encourage this interpretation. "Well said, well said!" the Buddha responds to Kasyapa's suggestion. "*From now on*, I do not permit my sravaka disciples to take flesh."[3]

. . .

This is an interesting historical question, but its only relevance today is that Buddhists who are addicted to meat—or who do not want to offend people addicted to meat—insist on trying to expand the Pali Canon almsbowl exemption to include purchased meat. By their logic, you could go into a chain restaurant like Red Lobster and order lobster off the menu with a clear conscience because the animal was frozen and had not been killed "specially for you." But you could not go into a more exclusive restaurant and pick out the lobster you wanted from the lobster tank. In the context of the Buddha's ethical teachings, this interpretation makes no sense. Either way, a lobster is killed and another is brought in to replace him, who will also be killed. Either way, you are responsible for the death of a sentient being.

The modern expansion of the ancient almsbowl exemption divorces the rule from its purpose. It allows people to claim that they are acting in accordance with the Buddha's teaching while they continue to indulge appetites that inflict suffering and death on sentient beings.

Except for the almsbowl exemption in the Pali Canon, both sets of scripture agree that the Buddha forbade his disciples to eat meat. *The Buddha's message to the modern world about meat is simple: Don't eat it.*

Mystery Meat

Buddhist defenders of meat-eating make their last stand at the Buddha's last meal, which they say included tainted pork that caused his death.

At 80 years of age, the Buddha had been seriously ill for some time and seemed to know that the hour of his passing into nirvana was approaching. Nevertheless, for reasons that are not explained, he left Magadha and in the course of his exodus stopped at the village of Pava, where he was invited to the home of a lay practitioner, a smith named Cunda. When they sat down to eat, the Buddha instructed his monks—with no further explanation—not to eat one of the dishes served by Cunda. But he ate it himself and then instructed Cunda to bury the leftovers so that no human or animal would eat them. That evening, he developed severe abdominal pain and diarrhea and began vomiting blood. Even so, the next morn-

ing, he insisted that they push on toward the village of Kushi-
nagara (Pali, Kusinara). On the road, he developed an unslak-
able thirst and had to stop frequently because of the diarrhea.
After an excruciating journey, they reached a park on the edge
of town, where the Buddha, weak and dehydrated, lay down
under a tree. Within hours, he was gone.

The *Mahaparinibbana Sutta*, which is part of the Pali
Canon, tells us that the Buddha became ill and died after eating *sukara-maddava* served him by his host.[4] *Sukara* means
"pig." *Maddava* has several meanings, most of which relate to
the ideas of "something to be eaten, food" "something soft,"
and "something enjoyable."[5] The word *sukara-maddava* was
apparently not in the vocabulary of early Buddhist commentators and so they had to guess at what it meant. Some took it
to mean "soft pig meat" and translated it "succulent pork" or
"minced pork," while others took it to mean "soft pig food" or
"pig's delight" and translated it "bamboo shoots" or "truffles,"
both of which are favorite foods of pigs.[6] For unknown reasons, some even thought that it meant "elixir," and was a
medicinal tonic that went tragically wrong.[7] The disagreement
continues to this day.

Damien Keown says that "the natural expression for 'pork'
in Pali would not be sukara-maddava but sukara-mamsa."[8]
Citing pioneering Buddhist scholar Carolyn Rhys-Davids,
who served for 20 years as president of the Pali Text Society,
Roshi Philip Kapleau makes the same point.[9] Kapleau also
quotes highly respected scholars K. E. Neumann and Arthur
Waley as pointing out that Pali includes "a whole series of
compound words having pig as their first element" that do not
refer to pork. Kapleau goes on to quote Waley as saying that
"Plant names tend to be local and dialectical," so that "sukara-
maddava" might mean truffles in Magadha but be incompre-
hensible elsewhere.[10] In his biography of the Buddha, *Old*

Path, White Clouds, Thich Nhat Hanh does not consider the controversy over sukara-maddava serious enough to even mention. Following ancient Chinese traditions, he says flatly of the meal served by Cunda, "It was a dish of mushrooms picked from a sandalwood tree and was called *sukara maddava*."[11]

In fact, we can be confident that sukara-maddava was not pork. In the passage from the *Jivaka Sutta* that I quoted earlier, the Buddha described in the most emphatic terms the negative karma that someone would incur who invited him or one of his disciples to dinner and served them meat. Knowing how strongly the Buddha felt about this, Cunda would not have done it. But even if somehow he had been unaware of the rule, there is no way that the Buddha would have permitted Cunda to inflict serious negative karma on himself by serving meat to him and his monks; nor is there any way that his attendant, the faithful Ananda, would have let that happen.

The *Mahaparinibbana Sutta* does not tell us why the Buddha ate the sukara-maddava. The traditional explanation that he did not want to hurt Cunda's feelings simply does not fly. First, the Buddha had no problem forbidding his monks to eat the lethal dish and telling Cunda to bury the rest of it so that not even animals would eat it. How could the Buddha have explained this bizarre procedure to Cunda without hurting his feelings? But, more importantly, had the Buddha declined the sukara-maddava because of his illness, that would have hurt Cunda's feelings far less than the knowledge that, however inadvertently, he had poisoned the Buddha and killed him. Even if the Buddha had not foreseen that the sukara-maddava would be fatal, which the sutta implies that he did, he would not have wanted to burden Cunda with the guilt of having made a sick old man sicker.

. . .

Viewed as history rather than hagiography, this is a very strange incident, beginning with the Buddha's hurried and unexplained departure from Magadha accompanied by only a small group of disciples. In her best-selling biography, *Buddha*, Karen Armstrong notes that some modern scholars[12] "have suggested that the Buddha realized that the *sukaramaddava* had been poisoned: they see the loneliness of the Buddha's end and the remoteness of the location as a sign of the distance between the Buddha and the Sangha and believe that, like the two old kings, he too died a violent death."[13]

This is not as far-fetched as it may appear. The schism of Devadatta was part of a wider generational power struggle in Magadha, in which the aging Buddha sided with his long-time friend and sponsor King Bimbisara, while the younger Devadatta sided with Bimbisara's son Prince Ajatashatru (Pali, Ajatasattu). In the end, the prince killed his father and seized the kingdom, which may explain why the Buddha left Magadha on his final journey without any of his closest followers in attendance except the ever-faithful Ananda. For the most part, the earliest followers of the Buddha had died ahead of him. Came the revolution, their successors may have not wanted to offend Ajatashatru once he held the power in Magadha.

Bimbisara was one of Armstrong's "two old kings." The other was King Pasanendi of neighboring Kosala, a friend of the Buddha and brother-in-law of Bimbisara, who was also overthrown by an impatient heir. Pasanendi died of vomiting and diarrhea (poison?) while fleeing for his life. Devadatta's fate is shrouded in mystery, but the Pali Canon suggests that he may have died before the Buddha, perhaps by his own hand. Even if this is so, the conservative faction in the Sangha would have survived him. We are told that the Buddha and Ajatashatru reconciled, but feigning remorse while plotting the Buddha's murder would be consistent with the new king's personality as it is portrayed in the Pali Canon. The interpretation by some early commentators of *sukara-maddava* as an "elixir" may disguise a memory of poison, distorted and denied because it was so unthinkable.

According to this theory, after the regicide of Bimbisara, the new king supported the conservatives in the sangha, who seized control from the Buddha and forced him to flee for his life. This theory—which, on the basis of evidence currently available, can neither be proved nor disproved—gains plausibility when we remember that according to the Pali Canon, Ajatashatru and Devadatta had conspired earlier in an unsuccessful plot to assassinate the Buddha.

If the Buddha was poisoned, we have no idea who administered the fatal dose. Cunda is a possibility, but so is an unknown household servant or one of the monks traveling with the Buddha, perhaps on an undercover mission to remove him from the scene. Likewise, we do not know why the Buddha took the poison, since he seemed to know it was there. Perhaps he really did not know until he had eaten it and the story was altered over the centuries. Or perhaps he hoped that his passing from the scene would remove an obstacle to harmony within the sangha. If so, this may be the real reason why he had refused to name a successor, believing that whether he chose a liberal or a conservative, the other faction would defect. Perhaps if they were forced to work by consensus, and neither party felt slighted, his followers would be able to hold the sangha together and avoid schism.

CHAPTER 8

A BRANCH OF SORROW

M eat-eating was not the only form of animal abuse specifically condemned by the Buddha. Tony Page observes that, "Of 16 deeds or practices which that Scripture [the Mahayana *Mahaparinirvana Sutra*] lists as 'evil' and to be shunned 'eternally'—no fewer than *13* concern the exploitation or ill-treatment of animals. These evil practices are:

1) keeping, feeding, and fattening sheep for profit and sale
2) buying and killing sheep for profit
3) raising, fattening, and killing pigs for profit
4) buying and killing pigs for profit
5) raising, fattening, and selling calves for profit
6) buying and killing calves for profit
7) raising hens for profit and selling them when fully grown
8) buying hens for profit and killing them
9) fishing
10) hunting

11) selling fish
12) catching birds by net, and
13) charming snakes."[1]

In addition to all forms of animal agriculture, this passage prohibits hunting, fishing, and fishmongering. In the modern world, the ban against catching wild birds can and should be extended to the capture of all wild animals for zoos, theme parks, and other uses. And, as Page points out, the injunction against snake charming effectively prohibits the use of performing animals in circuses, nightclub acts, or any other form of entertainment.[2]

Page goes on to say that he "knows of no passage in the Sutras which portrays the Buddha (Shakyamuni) as riding around on a horse or even a donkey (after his gaining of Enlightenment). He seems to have *walked* everywhere. Is this not itself testimony to his respect for animals?"[3] No doubt it is. But the Buddha gave up his horse not when he gained enlightenment, but when he fled his father's palace to pursue the life of an ascetic, and it seems likely that his walking was due at least as much to his avoidance of luxury as to his respect for animals. We have to acknowledge that the Buddha seems not to have objected to the use of animals for transportation or labor so long as they were not overworked or mistreated. He may well have believed that domesticated animals were happy if they were well cared for and allowed to live out their lives in peace when their productive years were behind them.

Orion Was Not a Buddhist
The Buddha prohibited hunting, and both Theravada and Mahayana consider hunting to be an activity in which Buddhists may not participate. This historic Buddhist position

was emphatically restated in an official proclamation issued by His Holiness the Dalai Lama in response to a request that I made on behalf of The Fund for Animals for a statement condemning trophy hunting in Mongolia. (Most Mongolians are Tibetan Buddhists.) His Holiness responded with the following official Appeal dated March 29, 2002, which I quote here in full:

> I am deeply saddened to learn that Mongolia encourages trophy hunting of rare and endangered species for tourism. We all know that taking others' lives is in general against Buddhist principles. How can we destroy and play with the lives of animals merely for fun, pleasure, and sport? It is unthinkable. Tibet, as a Buddhist country, in the past had banned hunting of animals in any form. Today there is greater awareness worldwide for the protection not only of the environment but also of animals, their rights, and their protection against torture. And therefore, even in countries where there are strong traditions of hunting, people are passing laws to ban it. A good case in point is the recent ban on fox hunting by the Scottish Parliament. I therefore appeal to all concerned in Mongolia not to indulge in trophy hunting of rare and endangered species. I make this appeal as a Buddhist because of our respect and compassion for all living beings.

In this Appeal, His Holiness makes four points that are of particular interest to us. First, hunting violates Buddhist "respect and compassion for all living beings." Second, environmental protection cannot be separated from the protection of individual living beings; hunting is not consistent with Buddhist environmentalism. Third, culture and tradition are not a justification for hunting, or any other kind of cruelty. And finally, outright prohibition, using the mechanisms of government if necessary, is an appropriate Buddhist response to the killing of animals when appeals to conscience and "mindfulness" fail to suffice.

Despite this unambiguous history, some prominent American Buddhists, such as poet and ecologist Gary Snyder, insist that hunting is compatible with the Buddhadharma. Their argument is put forward with unusual bluntness by Dr. Michael Soulé, a retired professor of conservation biology who is widely considered the founder of that discipline. Writing in *Tricycle*, Buddhist freelance writer Lisa Jones characterizes Soulé's view this way: "In the midst of today's extinction crisis, nonharming is synonymous with preserving biological diversity. For example, the removal of top predators [wolves and coyotes] from most ecosystems has caused skyrocketing populations of herbivores [she means deer and elk], with disastrous ecological consequences in many parts of the country."[4]

Before we proceed, I have to note that rising populations of deer and elk are due primarily to the policies of state wildlife agencies, which through most of the twentieth century deliberately promoted the growth of large herds of big game animals in order to sell more of the hunting licenses on which their budgets depend. While the removal of predators is certainly a factor—and was a shamefully misguided policy motivated by a combination of greed and fear—the hunting industry, including biologists in state wildlife agencies, is primarily responsible for the "skyrocketing populations of herbivores." Now, having deliberately created these populations to promote the sale of hunting licenses, state wildlife agencies tell the public that hunting is the only solution to this "overpopulation crisis." It is a disingenuous claim at best.[5] It is significant that there do not seem to be soaring populations of other animals, such as squirrels and rabbits, who also make meals for "top predators" but do not bring in big money to the wildlife agencies.

"So the way Soulé sees it," Jones continues, "it's preferable to put a dent in the exploding populations of deer and elk, rather than to eat industrially raised cattle, whose production requires enormous amounts of land, corn, water, and petroleum."[6] She then quotes Soulé's summation of his argument: "If by killing, we're enhancing diversity," he says, "then indeed that obligates us to kill."[7] This implication that the Buddhadharma "obligates us to kill" is a perversion of the Buddha's teaching. Soulé reveals himself here as a disciple of Angulimala, not the Buddha; he believes that killing is the path to happiness, an idea that the Buddha rejected unequivocally.

There are several problems with this claim, and as a Buddhist, Jones is well aware of the one that pops to mind first. "Why," she asks, "doesn't Soulé give up eating meat entirely?"[8] His answer is that "Modern [plant] agriculture gobbles up huge amounts of land and water—habitat that would be better utilized for wildlife, including escalating numbers of endangered species. . . . I think that everyone should try to eat ethically, to minimize one's footprint on the earth."[9]

Soulé's argument is flawed through and through. First, the notion that ethical eating places a higher priority on "minimizing one's footprint on the earth" than on not harming living beings may be the view of contemporary conservation biology, but it is not a view that can be reconciled with the Buddhadharma. The notion that we have an ethical obligation to kill if that "enhances biodiversity" represents a kind of ecological collectivism that is antithetical to Buddhist ethical teaching. Only individual sentient beings are able to suffer, and therefore, a compassion-based ethical system must always place the individual above the collective. The focus of Buddhist ethics is the individual living being, not the population or the ecosystem.

Secondly, there is no animal more overpopulated than human beings, no animal who causes anywhere near the environmental degradation that we cause, and no animal who represents anything remotely approaching the threat to biodiversity that we represent. Our footprint on the earth is that of an elephant while that of other species—including the deer and elk whom Soulé enjoys killing—is that of a flea. Nothing would enhance biodiversity nearly as much as killing large numbers of human beings. Does Michael Soulé believe that this undeniable fact "obligates us to kill" one another? If not, why does he believe that killing animals in the name of biodiversity is ethically acceptable? We have seen that in Buddhist teachings a "living being" is a living being, and the line which the Western intellectual tradition draws between the human and the nonhuman has no place. Killing animals in the name of biodiversity is a function of the Western hubris that believes we are able to "manage" nature. It is not genuine Buddhist teaching. We created our environmental problems by meddling in natural processes that we still understand very poorly. It is delusional to think that further meddling will solve them.

An authentically Buddhist ecology is based on the preservation and protection of the environment—plants, earth, air, and water—for the sole reason that this environment, in proper working order, is essential to sentient life. Buddhism teaches us that the individual living being is not simply a component of a "functioning ecosystem," interchangeable with every other member of his species and therefore expendable if he becomes inconvenient. He is a sentient being, entitled to the full protection of our compassion. We preserve the ecosystem to protect him; we do not kill him to protect the ecosystem.

Soulé's notion that hunting your food leaves a smaller footprint on the earth than eating vegetables gives a superficial appearance of validity only because he is improperly comparing the footprint of the individual hunter to the footprint of an agricultural industry that has to feed millions of people. If Soulé grew his own vegetables and fruits in an organic, hand-tended garden, his dietary footprint, so to speak, would be smaller than his footprint as a hunter. Conversely, if all 290 million people in the United States tried to feed themselves by hunting, their ecological footprint would be devastating and the edible species would quickly be blasted into the extinction that Soulé piously protests his hunting is intended to prevent. *A vegan diet is by far the most environmentally friendly diet possible, whether it is feeding one person or an entire population.* Small, organic fruit and vegetable farms scattered throughout the country and distributing their produce locally would represent the pinnacle of environmentally friendly eating, and of a society organized along Buddhist social principles. But unless and until that goal is achieved, any vegan or vegetarian diet is more compassionate, more respectful of the earth and all its living beings, and more consistent with Buddhist ideals than a diet based on animal products.

Blood Puja

Biomedical research on living beings—vivisection—would seem to be different from other forms of animal exploitation. The research is performed to cure disease and prevent suffering. It is undertaken out of compassion; therefore, it would appear to be done with virtuous intent.

But intent covers more than simply the goal. It also covers the means we choose to attain the goal. A basic teaching, common to all schools of Buddhism, is that we must not try to build our happiness on the suffering of others. In the passage from the *Dhammapada* that I quoted in the frontispiece, the Buddha said, "He who for the sake of happiness hurts others who also want happiness, shall not hereafter find happiness."[10] This theme is echoed in a classic Tibetan text on developing bodhichitta, *The Seven Points of Mind Training*, which cautions us against making our happiness a branch of someone else's sorrow. Or, as one contemporary teacher translates it, more straightforwardly, "Do not seek happiness by causing unhappiness to others."[11]

The modern world has no clearer instance of seeking happiness by causing unhappiness to others than biomedical research and product testing on animals. The fact that vivisectors may not anticipate benefiting personally from the research does not change this fact. They are trying to benefit the class of beings with whom they identify, humanity, at the cost of a class of beings whom they perceive as "other." What they are doing is contrary to Buddhist teachings on the unity of life.

Rick Bogle is co-founder and director (with Lynn Pauley) of the Primate Freedom Project, a California-based group that campaigns against biomedical experiments on great apes and monkeys. In 2001, Bogle saw a picture of the Dalai Lama touring a research laboratory at the University of Wisconsin in the company of Dr. Ned Kalin, a notorious vivisector, and emailed his concerns. He received this reply from Tenzin Geyche Tethong, personal secretary to the Dalai Lama.

Date: Thu, 06 Sep 2001
From: Office of His Holiness the Dalai Lama
Dear Rick Bogle,

Thank you for your e-mail letter of August 25 addressed to His Holiness the Dalai Lama. His Holiness appreciates your bringing to His attention the work of Dr. Ned Kalin. His Holiness was not aware that Dr. Kalin was involved in conducting tests on animals that were painful and extremely cruel. His Holiness has always been against such tests on animals. In fact, when His Holiness offered to make a contribution to research work by Dr. Paul Ekman on the subject of CULTIVATING EMOTIONAL BALANCE, His Holiness specifically pointed out that the research work should not involve experiments on animals.

> With Best Wishes,
> Tenzin Geyche Tethong[12]

. . .

In *Buddhism and Animals*, Tony Page observes that:

There was no developed and widespread practice of vivisection at the time of the Buddha. . . . There was, however, a good deal of animal sacrifice to the 'gods' in the belief that such sacrifices would bring blessings, health, and happiness. . . . There is a direct parallel with vivisection here, since today's lauded, sacrificing 'priests' (robed in white) are animal 'researchers'; their temple is their laboratory, and their slaughter of animals is most tellingly termed (by the vivisectors themselves) 'sacrifice.'[13]

Dr. Page has it exactly right. Vivisection is the modern equivalent of religious animal sacrifice, both being attempts to purchase our own well-being with the lives of animals.

According to Ashvaghosha (c. 130 CE), an Indian biographer of the Buddha who cannot be neatly categorized as either Theravada or Mahayana, the Buddha responded to a question about animal sacrifice by invoking the principle of not gaining happiness by causing suffering to another. "I desire not that fruit which is bought by causing pain to others! To kill a helpless victim through a wish for future reward, it would be an unseemly action for a merciful-hearted good man, even if the reward of the sacrifice were eternal."[14]

Mahathera Saddhatissa, the twentieth-century Theravadin sage whom I quoted earlier, put it most succinctly. "A Buddhist does not sacrifice living beings for worship or food, but sacrifices instead his own selfish motives."[15] Neither should a Buddhist sacrifice living beings for scientific knowledge or human health.

CHAPTER 9

PRECIOUS HUMAN BIRTH

In Chapter Three, I said that the Buddha nature of all sentient beings is identical and Buddhism teaches no hierarchy of beings such as has been so popular in Western thought. Even so, Buddhism considers birth as a human being extremely desirable and birth as an animal a misfortune. To understand this preference for human birth, we have to digress for a moment to take a look at the floor plan, so to speak, of samsara.

Samsara may be pictured as a six-story apartment building in which the residents are constantly moving from one apartment to another and from one floor to another.[1] The higher the floor, the less the residents living there suffer. They become eligible for a higher floor by accumulating positive karma, while negative karma sends them to one of the lower floors. The top floor is the realm of the *devas*. Although *deva* is usually translated "god," the devas are not gods as we in the West think of them, but simply living beings whose positive karma accumulated in past lives has earned them rebirth in a realm whose inhabitants enjoy a privileged existence filled with pleasure until the very end. The devas really do not suffer at all until death approaches and they realize with horror that they have exhausted their positive karma and will soon be reborn in a lower realm where they will suffer greatly.

The next floor down is the realm of the *asuras*, or "demigods," who would experience very little suffering were it not that they are jealous of the devas and waste their lives in angry, futile attempts to destroy the devas' happiness. Below the realm of the asuras is the human realm and below that the animal realm. Next comes the realm of the *pretas*, or "hungry ghosts," miserable beings who suffer constantly from hunger they cannot satisfy and thirst they cannot slake. Finally, in what we might think of as the basement, come the hell realms, where unfortunate beings suffer terrible, unrelenting torments until the negative karma that brought them there is exhausted and they are reborn in a higher realm. There are hot hells, cold hells (For Buddhists, it can literally be "cold as hell."), and hells where your body is constantly sliced open by razor-sharp swords. Here, it is instructive to note that if Buddhism regarded plants as sentient beings, there would be a "plant realm" located somewhere on this scale, but there is not because plants are not sentient beings and therefore not subject to suffering, karma, and rebirth.

Two of these realms, the human and the animal, are the visible realms, where you and I live and of which we are fully aware. The other four are the invisible realms, which we know of only because highly realized spiritual masters, who have seen them while deep in meditation, or who are able to remember them from past lives, have described them to us. The beings who inhabit the invisible realms share the same Buddha nature as those of us who live in the visible realms. As we journey through samsara we are all reborn in first one realm and then another, as we are blown from life to life, realm to realm by the "winds of karma." Positive karma leads us to rebirth in a higher realm with less suffering, and negative karma to a lower realm with worse suffering. None of these realms, however, is entirely satisfactory, first because none is permanent, and second because all entail some amount of suffering. Realms are "higher" or "lower" only according to the degree of suffering typically experienced in them. Genuine, enduring happiness can be found only in nirvana.

· · ·

The hierarchy of samsara is a hierarchy of suffering, not a hierarchy of beings. All inhabitants of samsara—which is to say, all sentient beings—are not simply equal, but are indistinguishable in their essential nature. The realms we inhabit are only temporary abodes, and as we travel on in search of enlightenment, we will move about from one to another as easily as moving from one floor to another in our imaginary apartment building.

In the analogy of the apartment, the resident is the Buddha nature, the apartment is the body and mind which that Buddha nature temporarily occupies, and the floor is the realm. The human body and mind that I have now are not me; they are part of the realm of samsara that I am inhabiting during this life; they are the links that bind my Buddha nature to the human realm. When I die and am reborn, my Buddha nature will be attached to whatever realm my karma sends it to by a body and/or mind appropriate to that realm.[2] Life in samsara is an interminable series of short-term rentals and disruptive moves from one substandard apartment to another that ends only when we gain enlightenment and vacate the building.

When Buddhist teachers say that the animal realm is

"lower" than the human realm, they are simply saying that life in the animal realm typically (although not always) entails greater suffering than life in the human realm. They are not saying that animals are inherently inferior to human beings or less entitled to our respect and our compassionate treatment. Quite the opposite, in fact, because the more a being needs our compassion, the greater is our obligation to offer it.

The more pervasive suffering of the animal realm is one reason why rebirth there is a misfortune for a human being and the result of negative karma. (There is also a second reason, which I will discuss in the next section.) For a hell being or a hungry ghost to be reborn in the animal realm would be good fortune and the result of positive karma because it would bring less suffering and even some opportunity for happiness.

The Land of Opportunity

Buddhist teachers often speak of a "precious human birth." And in Tibetan Buddhism, every sitting meditation session begins with a brief meditation on the rarity and incalculable value of such a birth. A human birth is not precious because of its freedom from suffering. As we just saw, on the suffering scale human birth ranks third in a field of six. There are two other options that are more desirable. Buddhism regards human birth as uniquely valuable because it presents an unparalleled opportunity to engage in spiritual practice and make progress toward nirvana. In this context, "precious" simply means "spiritually advantageous."

Not every human birth is precious, because not every human birth is conducive to spiritual progress. Even in the human realm, a precious birth is a rarity, greatly to be treasured and not to be wasted. A human birth is deemed precious only if it includes what are called the "Eight Freedoms" and "Ten Endowments." There is no need to list them here, but taken together they comprise the freedom, leisure, and health to engage in spiritual practice and the opportunity to encounter teachers who will guide us on the spiritual path. A human life that offers little opportunity to engage in spiritual practice is not a precious human birth.

The devas have such long lives filled with so much pleasure that they have no motivation to practice dharma until death approaches, when it is too late. The asuras are so obsessed by jealousy and hatred for the devas that they never give spiritual practice a thought. Animals are believed to lack the intellectual ability and the language necessary to work with abstract spiritual concepts or engage in practices such as meditation or mantra recitation. Pretas are so consumed by hunger and thirst that they can hardly think of anything else. And the poor hell beings must constantly endure agony so intense that even the briefest spiritual thought is said to be as rare as a pool of cool, clear water in a desert.

A precious human birth, on the other hand, entails enough suffering that we are motivated to engage in spiritual practice but not so much that we are precluded from it. A human mind, while not able to comprehend ultimate truth other than by direct intuition,[3] is capable of understanding the importance of spiritual practice and devising techniques for developing compassion and wisdom; human language is capable of transmitting a tradition of spiritual teaching from one person to another and one generation to another, and a precious human birth provides sufficient leisure to engage in the time-consuming practices of study, contemplation, and meditation.

Since human beings are only a tiny fraction of the total number of living beings in samsara, and only a tiny fraction of human beings enjoy the Freedoms and Endowments essential to spiritual practice, a precious human birth is to be treasured above any other form of birth in samsara. A precious human birth, therefore, is a fortunate external circumstance that is to be taken advantage of because it will soon be lost. It is not an essential characteristic of a living being that makes her superior to or entitled to better treatment than any other living being.

Noting that human birth typically provides greater opportunities for spiritual practice than animal birth, Kalu Rinpoche, a Tibetan high lama who played a major role in the 1960s and '70s in bringing the dharma to the West, draws this distinction between the human and animal realms. "Women and men, children and adults, all share, to some extent, the opportunities and freedoms of our human condition. By contrast, animals and those in other states of existence lack these opportunities and freedoms. The distinction between human and beast—wild carnivores living in the jungle, deep sea creatures or insect life—is made precisely on the basis of this opportunity to practice the Dharma."[4] In other words, we are not better than animals, we are just more fortunate in our present circumstances. And it is precisely because we are more fortunate that we owe them our compassion and our protection.

A Case of Projection

At this point we have to acknowledge that Buddhist teachers in general, and Tibetan teachers in particular, have an indefensibly low opinion of the intelligence of nonhuman animals. The following assessment by Kalu Rinpoche is typical of what Tibetan teachers have to say about life as a nonhuman animal. "In the animal realm stupidity and ignorance lead to blind instinctive behavior and to the preying of one species upon another."[5] The irony here is that nonhuman predators prey on other species because they are physiological carnivores. They have no other way to feed themselves. It is, in fact, humans who prey on one another and on other species out of "stupidity and ignorance."

Reginald Ray, professor of Buddhist studies at Naropa University in Boulder, Colorado, accurately reflects the Tibetan view when he says that "Animals are marked by a relative fixity of habitual patterns, dictated by the limitations of their nervous systems and physical bodies. According to Tibetan tradition, the animal-realm mentality is characterized by dullness, stupidity, and delusion. Animals are driven in their actions by a kind of blind instinct that lacks openness or flexibility."[6]

"Dullness," "stupidity," and "blind instinct" may (or may not, we really do not know) characterize earthworms, slugs, and jellyfish, but terms such as these do a gross injustice to more complex animals, including vertebrates and crustaceans. Like Kalu Rinpoche, Ray is actually describing human maladaptation, not normal animal behavior. To make this clear, all we need to do is translate his descriptions into the jargon of psychology: "Marked by a relative fixity of habitual patterns" would become, "maladaptive behaviors acquired in childhood as coping mechanisms." And "driven by blind instinct that lacks openness or flexibility" would equate to "engages in compulsive behavior that does not adapt to changed circumstances." Ray's description of animal intelligence is almost a textbook description of human neurosis. Over the centuries, Tibetan teachers have taken some of the worst characteristics of human behavior and projected them onto nonhuman animals.

However much we may regret this denigration of animal intelligence, we must be careful not to read too much into it. Western students—who come out of a tradition that regards reason, intelligence, and language as the touchstones of individual worth and moral standing—typically interpret these stereotypes as denials of the inherent worth and moral standing of nonhuman animals. But this is a mistake. In Buddhism, including the Tibetan tradition, Buddha nature, not intelligence, is the touchstone of worth; and sentience, not reason, is the touchstone of moral standing. The Tibetan Buddhist attitude toward animals is not one of contempt or disparagement, but of compassionate concern for those less fortunate. Nonhuman animals are living beings like any other who, because of their negative karma, suffer greatly in a state of relative ignorance and impotence. It is incumbent upon Buddhists—indeed, upon all human beings—to use our intelligence and power to relieve as much of their suffering as we are able, and certainly not to add to it by our greed and cruelty.

We have already seen Geshe Rabten say that animals are "beings like us," and Kalu Rinpoche say that "The distinction between human and beast is made precisely on the basis of this opportunity to practice the Dharma." Variations in intelligence among species are of no more moral significance than variations in intelligence among individual human beings. Deshung Rinpoche[7] (1906–1987), one of the most respected Tibetan teachers of the twentieth century, observes that "Even in Tibet, you can find many Tibetans who are very fond of animals and always treat them with great kindness, but you will also find many who don't think twice about eating animals, as well as those who raise animals, treat them very lovingly, and in the end slaughter them. However humans generally respond to animals, the point is that, as Buddhists, we need to be very clear about how we relate to animals and all other beings, but especially to animals, who are karmically in a very unfortunate state. Compared to us, they are very handicapped. At the very least, we cannot countenance causing harm to other living creatures. As Buddhists we know that it is admirable and desirable that we develop compassion for all beings, including animals, to the utmost of our abilities. This is at the very heart of Buddhist practice."[8] Animals are our less fortunate brothers and sisters—less fortunate because less powerful and therefore more at the mercy of nature, other animals, and, worst of all, human beings. Whether that impotence is due to the anatomy of their bodies or the functionality of their brains is of no consequence. We are their stronger siblings, and it is incumbent upon us to use our power to protect them.

Obstruction of Karma

Frequently I am told in smug tones by meat-eating Western Buddhists that the suffering of animals is due to their karma. Since this is hardly a late-breaking news bulletin, my response is usually something along the lines of, "And your point is?" Their point is invariably the same. "If the karma of animals is to be raised on factory farms and slaughtered, it would be wrong for us to interfere by refusing to eat meat or wear leather."[9]

This objection is based on a fundamental misunderstanding of the law of karma, a misunderstanding that arises from viewing it through a theistic, Judeo-Christian lens. The Judeo-Christian model is social. We sin by violating laws handed down by a divine lawgiver, who will judge and punish us just as if we were in a civil courtroom for violating a criminal law. The Buddhist model is organic. The law of karma is a natural law, like Newton's third law of motion or the law of gravity; it is not a legislated law, such as laws against kidnapping, tax fraud, and driving on the wrong side of the street. It is *descriptive* rather than *prescriptive*, and it is certainly not *proscriptive*. The law of karma does not forbid us to do anything, nor does it instruct us to do anything. It simply describes the natural process of cause and effect that determines the consequences of our actions, just as the law of gravity describes the natural process that determines the consequences of stepping off a 10-story building into thin air.

. . .

The premise of the law of karma is that the universe is not merely physical, but also moral. Cause and effect governs the moral universe in the same way that it governs the physical universe. And just as there is natural law that governs the physical aspects of our actions, there is natural law that governs the moral aspects of our actions. The Dalai Lama describes karma as "an instance of the general law of causality. What makes karma unique is that it involves intentional action, and therefore, an agent. . . . In order for a causal process to be a karmic one, it must involve an individual whose intention would lead to a particular action."[10] Just as the law of gravity comes into play when two physical bodies come sufficiently close to one another, the law of karma comes into play when someone performs an intentional act that has the potential to harm or help a living being.

When we think of natural laws, we tend to think of mechanical laws, and the two examples I used above—Newton's third law of motion and the law of gravity—were both drawn from physics. But in fact, the law of karma is most often described in organic rather than mechanical terms. Mechanical analogies are not wrong; they illustrate the abstract concept quite accurately. But in actual operation, karma is more subtle and less straightforward than mechanical examples might suggest. The analogy that Buddhist teachers most often use is that of a seed. An action is a seed—or, more precisely, the intention that motivates an action is a seed—and just as acorns will never yield anything but oak trees and barley seed will never yield anything but barley, so a compassionate action will never yield anything but beneficial results for the person who commits it, and a selfish or cruel action will never yield anything but suffering. But just as a seed needs the proper conditions to ripen—good soil, moisture, sunshine, and the like—so does karma, which will not ripen until the proper conditions obtain, nearly always in some future lifetime. In fact, the biggest single effect of karma is to determine in which realm and in what circumstances we will be reborn. The reason why it is often true that "the wicked prosper and the good are destitute" is that in this life we are eating fruit that has grown from seeds that we planted in past lives, and so we are unable to see the connection between cause and effect.

. . .

Let's go back to our example of the law of gravity. If a baby fell from a window, no one would refuse to catch him on the grounds that we shouldn't interfere with the law of gravity. We would immediately recognize that such a claim is ridiculous. It is just as ridiculous to refuse to alleviate suffering because doing so would interfere with the law of karma. Everything that happens to us is in large measure the result of our karma. If we were to follow this "noninterference" theory, we would never help anyone in distress. Refusing to "interfere" with karma would leave no place for compassionate action in the world, a notion that is the antithesis of Buddhist teaching.

Cruelty in the Guise of Kindness

A more sophisticated version of the same objection goes like this: "These beings were born in the animal realm and on factory farms because of their negative karma. Sooner or later, this karma will have to ripen. It is kinder to let it ripen now so they can get it behind them and move on to a more fortunate rebirth without that old negative karma still hanging over their heads."

Unless we are highly realized beings, we have no way of

knowing our own karma, much less that of another being, and even less the karma of someone whom we never met while he was still alive. To condone—and even to participate in—cruelty to living beings under the guise that in order to work out their karma they need to suffer and die to provide the meat, leather, milk, and eggs that we enjoy is both arrogant and disingenuous. No one appointed us to be karma cops and enforce the law of karma. In fact, we can't enforce the law of karma: first, because it's not the kind of law that can be enforced—Can you imagine someone leaning against a wall and claiming that he was "enforcing" Newton's third law of motion?—and second, because we have no idea how the law of karma applies in any given situation or what a being's future karma may be. When we involve ourselves in the suffering of others, it should always be to relieve the suffering that we are aware of, never to inflict suffering on them now so that they might avoid some hypothetical suffering in future lives. Buddhas and highly realized bodhisattvas and arhats can do this because they have omniscience, but not the rest of us. What for holy beings is skillful means, for the rest of us is clumsy mucking around.

Suppose you have been involved in a serious accident on a deserted country road. You are lying on the side of the road beside the mangled wreckage of your car, broken and bleeding, when I drive by, stop, and get out. I look down at you and say, "I have a cell phone, but it's obviously your karma to die this early death. If I call 911 and the paramedics save you, you'd still have that old negative karma hanging over your head. So out of kindness, I'm going to leave you here to die; that way, you can have a favorable rebirth and get on with your spiritual journey. Oh, and by the way, since you won't be needing them, I'm going to take your Rolex and the $500 in your wallet."

We should always beware of arguments that justify the suffering of others on the grounds that it is for their own good, and never more than when the person making the argument benefits from the suffering. These are the arguments of selfishness, not compassion. We should also beware of arguments that justify the suffering and death of animals when those same arguments would never be used to justify the suffering and death of human beings. These are the arguments of speciesism, not Buddhism.

Animal Liberation

"The most beneficial of all composite roots of virtue is the protection and ransoming of the lives of sentient beings. A variety of that is saving the lives of livestock, which frees those animals from present danger to their lives."[11] These are the words of Jamgon Kongtrul Lodro Thaye (1813–1899), a leader of the nonsectarian (*rime*, ree-may) movement that revitalized Tibetan Buddhism in the second half of the nineteenth century, and universally recognized as one of Tibet's greatest spiritual masters. He is talking about a practice that is common to most schools of Buddhism, the liberation of condemned animals.

Although the details vary from one tradition to another, the essential practice typically includes three elements: 1) rescuing one or more animals who are doomed to an early death; usually, this is done by purchasing animals destined to be slaughtered for food or worms being sold as bait for fishing; 2) performing a ceremony or meditation practice intended to strengthen the practitioner's compassion; and 3) releasing the animals in a secure environment or placing them in a good home so that they may live out their lives in peace and safety.

Animal liberation practices serve three purposes: they alleviate the suffering of sentient beings; they promote the practitioner's spiritual growth; and they generate positive karma, which may help to prolong your life or the life of someone to whom you dedicate the liberation.[12] When the Dalai Lama was ill in an Indian hospital in 2002, Lama Zopa Rinpoche, director of the Foundation for the Preservation of the Mahayana Tradition (FPMT), a worldwide network of Tibetan meditation centers, called upon Buddhists everywhere to conduct animal liberation practices dedicated to the long life of His Holiness. FPMT reported that well-wishers liberated more than one million animals in response to Zopa Rinpoche's request.[13]

If it were compassionate to allow animals to suffer and die at the hands of human beings so that they could work out their negative karma, there would be no compassion, and therefore no merit, in animal liberation practices. But these practices are taught in all of the major traditions of Buddhism and are considered extremely virtuous.

CHAPTER 10

THE CABBAGE AND THE COW

A s we saw in Chapter Four, Western defenders of animal exploitation often claim that genuine consciousness—and therefore, the ability to suffer as we do—is found only in human beings. Buddhists sometimes go to the opposite extreme. In the Introduction, I quoted Bodhin Kjolhede's comment that American Buddhists sometimes justify meat-eating by equating the life of a cow with the life of a carrot. In his 1999 book *Celebrating Everyday Life*, popular Zen teacher, writer, and ecologist John Daido Loori counsels us that, "Because food is life, it is of utmost importance that we receive it with deepest gratitude. When we eat, we consume life. Whether it's cabbage or cows, it's life."[1]

This raises the question, "To whom, precisely, should our gratitude be directed?" The cabbage couldn't care less. In fact, it doesn't care at all. The cabbage has no nervous system and no brain. It is not physiologically equipped to have any kind of mental life, including the experience of pain. And from an evolutionary standpoint, there is no reason why it should be.

Since cabbages are incapable of discretionary activity, sentience has no survival or reproductive value for them. In the case of the cabbage, there is no one to whom we can offer our gratitude.

We could, of course, offer our gratitude to the cow whose flesh is the steak on our dinner plate. But what are we being grateful for? She was not a volunteer. She had to be dragged quite literally kicking and screaming to slaughter. Farmed animals are not future Buddhas donating their flesh out of compassion for those of us who have developed a craving for it. They are victims of our greed from whom we steal the most precious gift any of us has: life. If you were kidnapped, slaughtered, and eaten by space aliens whose power over us was as absolute as our power over the animals, would you think that act of murder was redeemed by the gratitude of the aliens? Or would you think the aliens were adding insult to injury?

But perhaps Loori is not talking about directing our gratitude to the plant or animal we are eating. Perhaps he is talking about a generalized feeling of appreciation that has no specific object. Buddhist teachers sometimes speak of "compassion without an object," by which they mean compassion so highly developed that it has become the person's abiding nature and does not need to encounter a specific instance of suffering to be triggered, just as the sun is by nature warm and bright and would shine whether or not it were shining *on* anything. Perhaps Loori is recommending "gratitude without an object."

"Compassion without an object" is simply another way to describe universal compassion for all sentient beings without discriminating among them on the basis of our attractions and aversions. "Gratitude without an object" is a way for practitioners to feel good about themselves while committing acts that violate their fundamental spiritual principles. We must eat to live, and we must eat "living things" because our bodies cannot survive on minerals. And if the cabbage and the cow are equal because "Whether it's cabbage or cows, it's life," then it is no more wrong to eat the cow than the cabbage. So if we enjoy London broil, there is no ethical reason to eat tofu instead. The equation of the cabbage and the cow constitutes tacit permission to eat the cow.

But the equation is false because it declares the cabbage and the cow to be equal on the basis of a trait that is irrelevant to their claim on our compassion: life narrowly defined as the ability to grow and reproduce. But the only quality that matters for compassion is sentience. If a being can suffer, it needs our compassion. If it cannot, it does not. It is not life *per se* that confers moral standing—the right to be treated with compassion—it is sentience. The cow suffered in the unnatural confinement of the factory farm; the cabbage did not suffer in the field. The cow suffered in the cattle car and the slaughterhouse; the cabbage did not suffer in the truck or the warehouse. The cow loved life and dreaded death; the cabbage was capable of neither love nor fear. Therefore, it is wrong to eat the cow—no matter how much "gratitude" we feel—and it is not wrong to eat the cabbage.

· · ·

In the spirit of ancient Chinese Buddhist traditions, Thich Nhat Hanh amplifies the First Precept this way. "Aware of the suffering caused by the destruction of life, I am committed to cultivating compassion and learning ways to protect the lives of people, animals, plants, and minerals."[2] The entire thrust of Thich Nhat Hanh's ethical teaching is to reduce the suffering and death that we inflict upon sentient beings, from the greatest to the tiniest, to the absolute minimum possible, as when he cautions us, "We may be killing every day by the way we eat, drink, and use the air, land, and water. We think that we don't kill, but we do."[3]

Nhat Hanh himself practices a compassionate vegetarian diet, and he requires each of the monks and nuns ordained into his order to take this vow: "Aware of the need to maintain good health, to live in harmony with the Sangha, and to nourish compassion in my heart, I vow to be vegetarian for the whole of my life and not to eat apart from the Sangha except when I am sick."[4] He directs the members of his robed Sangha, "When you are invited to a meal [in the home of a layperson], do not sit at a table where there is wine or meat."[5] Nhat Hanh's universal compassion is all the more admirable because it is existentially grounded in a life dedicated with unflagging courage to the practice of ahimsa despite persecution, war, and exile.

And yet, among his Western students, Nhat Hanh's compassionate lifestyle is not universally emulated. Some with whom I have spoken seem to regard vegetarianism as a kind of ritual purification practice that they follow only when they are on retreat or visiting the meditation center, while others cite their teacher's reformulation of the First Precept and make the argument of the cabbage and the cow. Nhat Hanh intends his expansion of the Precept to extend the principle of ethical responsibility to the environment. But to some of his Western students, it seems a convenient excuse for denying ethical treatment to animals.

Empti(headed)ness

In addition to the cow and the carrot, the other defense of meat-eating—and by extension animal killing—that I quoted from Bodhin Kjolhede's *Tricycle* article was the argument from emptiness, which asserts that "ultimately there is no killing and no sentient being being killed." Since this will sound like nonsense to non-Buddhists (Actually, it *is* nonsense, but I'll get to that soon enough.), we need to take at look at the doctrine of emptiness.

According to the teachings on emptiness, everything that we perceive with our senses lacks real, inherent existence. We know that this is true because nothing is permanent; everything is constantly in flux, transforming from one state to another. Things may transform very rapidly, like ice cubes melting under a hot faucet, or they may transform very slowly, like mountain ranges wearing down over many thousands of years; but they are, in one way or another, at one pace or another, transforming. Furthermore, if we view things from different points of view or under different conditions, they appear differently to us. A piece of paper that is white in white light, turns red in red light and blue in blue light. A piece of metal that appears solid to the touch and the human eye is seen under an electron microscope as a collection of discrete particles separated by vast amounts of empty space. Nothing in the perceptible world has a true nature independent of its surroundings and the perspective of the viewer. In Buddhist terminology, all phenomena are empty of inherent existence.

In the past century, the ancient Buddhist doctrine of emptiness has received unexpected confirmation from the findings of modern physics. Fred Alan Wolf, author of *The Spiritual Universe: How Quantum Physics Proves the Existence of the Soul*, told interviewer Julie Knowles that Sir Arthur Eddington, one of the founders of quantum mechanics, once remarked, "Here I am, sitting at a table, writing this paper. However, when I describe this 'real' table in the language of science as I understand it, it is a ghost; in fact it is made of atoms that are themselves mostly empty space."[6] Eddington himself is reputed to have said, "A thing is merely a specific class of events," which is not far removed from the Buddha's analysis of phenomena as empty of inherent existence. In fact, the phenomenal world described by the Buddha and the world described by modern physics have far more in common with each other than either has with the world of common sense.

There is, to be sure, a foundation of true, eternal, unchanging reality behind this phenomenal emptiness, but neither our senses nor our conceptual thought is capable of grasping it. As we said earlier, the Ultimate Reality can be approached only by the direct intuition that is accessed through meditation and other spiritual practices. In Mahayana language, the perceptual world that is empty of inherent existence is called "conventional reality," or sometimes "relative truth," while the underlying, genuine reality is known as "ultimate reality" or "ultimate truth." To use a vocabulary that we introduced earlier, conventional reality is samsara and ultimate reality is nirvana. Taken together, the "Two Truths," as they are known, describe the universe insofar as it can be described.

Peter Harvey says that emptiness "refers to reality as being ultimately incapable of being pinned down by concepts."[7] To put it more explicitly, emptiness does not deny that things exist; it simply denies that they exist *as we perceive them*. It denies, in other words, that we can ever understand the true nature of things except by the insight that comes with enlightenment. Until we achieve that insight, the doctrine of emptiness serves as a kind of *via negativa* or *neti, neti* that tells us what reality is not, so that we can loosen our attachment to the illusions of the senses and free our minds to pursue the intuitive, unitive knowledge that is enlightenment.

Emptiness is a transitional understanding of reality that helps us reach ultimate truth. It is a skillful means taught by the Buddha to carry us from ignorance to enlightenment, from samsara to nirvana. In interpreting the Buddha's teachings, we must always remember that he never showed any interest in describing the world in a philosophical way. He was not an Indian Plato or Aristotle; in his view, the pursuit of knowledge for its own sake was a waste of precious time. His only concern was to help us escape from this world of suffering in which we are trapped.

· · ·

The argument from emptiness that Sensei Kjolhede alludes to goes like this: "Since nothing has any inherent reality, the cow who is killed is not real, the killer is not real, nor is the act of killing real. Therefore, there has been no killing, nothing has been killed, and no harm has been done." Ignoring, for the moment, the fact that this argument is as silly from a Buddhist perspective as from any other, it rests on a fundamental misuse of the doctrine of emptiness.

The argument from emptiness uses the language of ultimate truth to describe relative truth, and in so doing commits a kind of category mistake. It is perfectly true that in the ultimate sense there is no cow, no killer, and no killing. It is just irrelevant, because in the relative sense, all three exist, and the cow experiences fear, pain, and death that either are real or seem real, a distinction far more important to meat-eating philosophers than to the cow. Relative truth is still truth—even though it is not the ultimate truth—and those of us who are trapped in samsara, including you, me, and the cow, are bound by it and subject to it. To beings trapped in samsara, the experiences of samsara are real, even though in an ultimate sense the phenomena that prompt those experiences may not be. Earlier, we compared samsara to a nightmare from which there is no escape except enlightenment. While we are experiencing it, the suffering of a nightmare is real. When we wake up, we realize that the mental images that caused our suffering were not real, but the suffering itself was real and it remains real in our memory. The suffering of samsara is no different.

The argument from emptiness treats a teaching device, a proposition intended to aid our minds in their search for enlightenment, as if it were a guide to conduct—something it was never intended to be. As we have seen, the Buddha's guides to conduct are very clear on the subject of killing, or causing any harm, to living beings, and they do not justify it on the grounds that it's okay because in an ultimate sense, it doesn't really happen. They tell us in unmistakable terms to be strict practitioners of ahimsa.

Speaking of the uses and misuses of the Two Truths, Thich Nhat Hanh warns us against getting "caught in theories or ideas, such as saying that 'suffering is an illusion' . . . . When you have a headache, it would not be correct to call your headache illusory. To help it go away, you have to acknowledge its existence and understand its causes."[8] And when a cow, a pig, or a fish is being killed, it is just as incorrect to call the killing illusory.

. . .

This brings us to the silliness of the argument from emptiness. One Sunday morning, I was standing in the kitchen of our meditation center pouring a cup of tea when another student, who had just learned I was vegan, came in. "You know," he said, "Vegetarianism reflects a very superficial understanding of Buddhism." "Really?" I said, "How so?" And he gave me the argument from emptiness. I reached over and picked up a long, serrated kitchen knife that was lying on the counter. I tested the edge of the blade with my finger and asked him to stretch his neck out and lean his head over the sink so the blood wouldn't mess up the floor. His eyes grew wide, his Adam's apple bobbed up and down, and he sputtered for a moment. He didn't know me well—and, after all, I was an animal rights fanatic—maybe I was just crazy enough to actually slit his throat. "What are you worried about?" I asked. "After all, in the ultimate sense, you don't exist, I don't exist, and my act of killing you won't exist. So there's no problem, right?" He glared at me for a moment, then turned and left the kitchen muttering, "You just don't understand Buddhism." "One of us certainly doesn't," I thought. But I wanted him to spend his drive home thinking about the point I had made, not plotting how he would one-up me next Sunday, so I kept that thought to myself.

The Buddha's statement in the *Dhammapada*, "See yourself in others," is the Buddhist litmus test for ethical claims. Any defense of killing that we would not use to defend the killing of ourselves if our situations were exchanged is not a valid argument for killing another sentient being.

When Is a Rule Not a Rule?

When I tell people that eating meat violates the First Precept, they sometimes remind me that the Precepts are not hard and fast rules, like a civil law or the Ten Commandments; they are guidelines for training the mind. While we should follow them as closely as we can, these people say, we should not feel guilty about lapses or even consistent failures. And we most certainly should not presume to tell other people how they should keep the precepts. That would show a most un-Buddhist lack of compassion and a misunderstanding of the nature of the precepts.

Once again, we are encountering an argument that sets a different standard for our conduct toward animals than toward humans, a disparity that has no justification in Buddhist teachings. A trivial interest of the meat-eater (annoyance, hurt feelings) is placed above the vital interests of the animals whose flesh he eats (life, liberty, and the integrity of their bodies). This is speciesism, pure and simple. Would any Buddhist suggest that the First Precept does not forbid us to kill and eat human beings, but merely points us in the direction we should be moving? Would any Buddhist suggest that it would show a lack of compassion to criticize Jeffrey Dahmer for his serial killing and cannibalism? Where other human beings are concerned, the Precept does not point us in the direction of not killing them, it does not remind us to kill them mindfully, with gratitude and respect, it forbids us to kill them, and it similarly forbids the killing of animals.

We should certainly feel compassion for Jeffrey Dahmer; we should forgive him his sins; and, if we had had the opportunity, we should have tried to help him onto the spiritual path. But surely our compassion should never have extended to a refusal to criticize serial murder and cannibalism. Jeffrey Dahmer killed 15 people over a 13-year period. Americans who eat meat, eggs, and dairy share responsibility for the killing of 130 billion sentient beings in a like period. Compassion demands that we speak out, not keep silent, in the face of an ongoing atrocity of this magnitude. Thich Nhat Hanh tells us, "If we see social injustice, when we practice non-action we may cause harm. When people need us to say or do something, if we don't, we can kill by our inaction or our silence."[9]

The Precepts are guidelines for training, rather than hard and fast rules, because, as we said earlier, they are expressions of the great compassion, instructions for putting it to work in the world. As such, they prohibit behavior that is inherently callous or cruel. The fact that they are not a legalistic system of regulations does not mean that we are free to behave callously or cruelly—by eating meat, for instance—with a free conscience. In fact, just the opposite: It means that we cannot use a strict interpretation of the guidelines to justify acting in an uncompassionate way. We live by the spirit of the precepts or we do not live by them at all. As we saw when we examined the Buddha's attitude toward eating meat, we cannot sneak by on a technicality, because there are no technicalities. In Buddhist ethics, the letter exists to point us toward the spirit. Divorced from the spirit, it loses its meaning. In the Christian tradition, Saint Paul said, "The letter of the law kills, but the spirit gives life."[10] That is nowhere more true than in Buddhism.

CHAPTER II

MORE MIND GAMES

One popular approach to the question of meat-eating is to deflect the discussion away from the suffering of the animals and onto the supposed "intolerance" of anyone who criticizes it. There are infinite variations on this theme, but the point is made with particular clarity by Sister Chan Khong, a nun who has been one of Thich Nhat Hanh's closest associates for more than three decades. She writes, "Some vegetarians are too extreme, and are unkind to those who cannot give up meat-eating. I am more comfortable with a meat-eater than an extremist vegetarian who is filled with self-righteousness."[1]

Before dealing with the question at hand, I first must agree with Sister Chan Khong that anger is a negative emotion without redeeming value. Anger does immeasurable harm to everyone it touches and generates the worst kind of karma, rebirth as a hell being. It is always a corrosive state of mind and a treacherous motivator. Nothing worthwhile can be accomplished through anger that cannot be accomplished better through lovingkindness and compassion.

That said, the notion that a laid back meat-eater is a better embodiment of peace and a better practitioner of ahimsa than an intense vegetarian reveals a strange notion of violence. Meat kills—it kills 48 billion land animals every year. The idea that the level of violence implicit in a vegetarian's anger over that atrocity is somehow comparable to the violence inherent in factory farming and animal slaughter is misguided. What those who make this claim are really saying is that they have to experience the vegetarian's anger, and it makes them uncomfortable—in part, I suspect, because they know she is right. But they do not have to experience the violence of the slaughterhouse, and they have grown comfortable hiding behind their willful ignorance. Whether they are meat-eaters themselves or simply unwilling to confront meat-eaters, their solution to the suffering of animals at the hands of humans is to silence its critics, so that their own sense of well-being will remain undisturbed. They have never learned the difference between peace and comfort.[2]

But Sister Chan Khong is not talking exclusively about anger. She is also condemning the claim that vegetarianism is a more virtuous diet than meat-eating, which she scathingly characterizes as "self-righteousness." But in reality, vegetarianism *is* a more virtuous diet than meat-eating; it causes less suffering. And the relief of suffering is the whole point of Buddhist virtue. The refusal to criticize flesh eating because doing so would be "unkind" (in Chan Khong's term) to the flesh eater is tantamount to refusing to criticize murder because that would unkind to the murderer. It is committing a felony to avoid a misdemeanor.

Chan Khong alludes to those who "cannot" give up meat-eating. With the possible exception of a small percentage of people with severe metabolic deficiencies—people who suffer from a pathology—there is no one in the industrialized world who cannot give up meat-eating and who would not be healthier for it. But there are a lot of people in the industrialized world who do not want to give up their addiction to meat; and like alcoholics and drug addicts, meat addicts are masters of self-deception. They convince themselves that without their daily fix of dead flesh they become listless and experience a nonspecific but debilitating malaise. Defenders of meat-eating have even created a "failure to thrive syndrome" (FTS), and suggested—with no evidence—all sorts of biochemical causes.

. . .

Philip Glass, perhaps America's most celebrated living composer of classical music and film scores and a Tibetan Buddhist practitioner, seems to think that physical meat dependency is the common state of humanity and vegetarians like himself are exceptions to the norm. "You need physical stamina to undertake this [a vegetarian diet], and, if you have it, count it as a blessing."[3] Why? "A vegetarian diet often results in various ailments and general weakness for even the most nutrition-conscious. . . . [G]iving up animal products entirely invites health problems for most people. Because this is not generally admitted, people have a vague feeling of guilt about their diets. . . . And guilt has no place here. After all, how can you hope to work toward the benefit of all living beings if the way you are living makes you too weak or sick to do anything useful?"[4]

This is nonsense from beginning to end. According to Dr.

Michael Klaper, a physician who has studied human nutrition for three decades:

> The human body has absolutely no requirement for animal flesh. Nobody has ever been found face-down 20 yards from the Burger King because they couldn't get their Whopper in time.[5]

The American Dietetic Association (ADA) is the primary professional association of American nutrition professionals; its counterpart group in Canada is Dietitians of Canada. Both are conservative organizations not given to endorsing fads or jumping on bandwagons. In June 2003, the Journal of the ADA published an article on vegetarianism in which the two groups took the following official position:

> It is the position of the American Dietetic Association and Dietitians of Canada that appropriately planned vegetarian diets are healthful, nutritionally adequate, and provide benefits in the prevention and treatment of certain diseases.[6]

Anyone who may suffer from a genuine metabolic pathology should have his or her condition diagnosed and treated by a physician, where appropriate with the help of a nutritionist. But in the vast majority of cases, I believe that FTS "victims" are like the young boy in Thomas Mann's novel *The Confessions of Felix Krull, Confidence Man* who, when he wanted to stay home from school, would pretend to be sick and enter so completely into his act that he would actually feel the symptoms of illness. These folks do not want to stop eating meat, and so they convince themselves that they cannot. And as long as we—in the name of "kindness," "compassion," and "toler-ance"—refuse to condemn the cruelty that is integral to meat-eating, they will never be motivated to make a serious effort.

. . .

Michael Soulé, the conservation biologist whom I quoted earlier in connection with hunting, puts a post-modernist, politically correct twist on Sister Chan Khong's argument about "self-righteousness."

> We humans embrace polarization as if it were better than sex. Take a look at any social movement. Internal struggles predominate. Usually the purists are fighting with the pragmatists. Animal rights advocates hate the animal welfarists, conservationists dismiss the promot-ers of sustainable development, vegans disparage vege-tarians. When I look around, I see fundamentalism all the way down.[7]

Notice that in each of Soulé's examples, the "polarization" is blamed entirely on the "purists." "Animal rights advocates," for example, "hate the animal welfarists," but there is no men-tion of welfarists responding in kind. Reading this, I had to wonder what Michael Soulé would have said about the anti-slavery movement had he been alive in the 1850s. Would he have accused Frederick Douglass, William Lloyd Garrison, Sojourner Truth, Henry David Thoreau, and their fellow abo-litionists of being "purists" and "fundamentalists"? Would he have sided with the "pragmatists" who wanted to purchase the freedom of individual slaves but who thought that the aboli-tion of slavery was too radical and impractical an approach?

Like many Western Buddhists, Soulé misses the critical

point. The animal rights movement is no more about the activists than the abolition movement was about the abolitionists. The abolition movement was about the suffering and the end of the suffering of slaves, and the animal rights movement is about the suffering and the end of the suffering of animals.

The Argument from Mindfulness

In all schools of Buddhism, mindfulness is a central practice. Techniques vary, but they are all intended to help us "abide in the present moment," alert to where we are, what we are doing, and why we are doing it. Within the scheme of dharma practice, mindfulness serves three purposes: First, it helps us achieve mental stability and thereby aids our meditation. Second, it weakens our attachment to the objects of desire and aversion, helping us to achieve wisdom. Finally, by sharpening our awareness of our behavior and the motivations behind it, mindfulness helps us to develop compassion.

The argument from mindfulness is sometimes invoked to defend hunting, fishing, and eating meat (all practices condemned by the Buddha), and it goes something like this. "If I hunt, fish, or eat meat mindfully, with a respectful and compassionate awareness of the suffering of the animal, and the wish that she enjoy a favorable rebirth, then it's okay."

It is not okay. When we respect someone, we respect his or her needs and interests; most especially we respect his or her love of life. Killing innocent beings because we enjoy the taste of their flesh is inherently disrespectful. The Buddha said, "Our life is the creation of our mind."[8] A compassionate mind will create a compassionate lifestyle, including a compassionate choice of food.

When virtuous mental attitudes, like mindfulness, respect, and compassion, are invoked to justify nonvirtuous acts like hunting, fishing, and eating animal products, the mental attitudes are insincere. They are self-deceptions that we create to justify habits that in our hearts we know are wrong, but to which we have become attached. If eating the meat, drinking the milk, or eating the eggs were necessary to sustain our lives, and we did so only reluctantly, regretfully, and with the sincere wish that there were some way, any way, that we could stay alive without causing the death of other beings, then our mindfulness would, in fact, be virtuous. But we do not need their flesh, milk, and eggs in order to survive. In fact, we would be healthier without them. We consume the lives of animals because we enjoy the taste and texture of animal products. If we are being honest about it, when we eat animal products, we kill for pleasure, and in that circumstance our mindfulness is a sham. It is a self-deception that we use to quiet our consciences while we continue to sin unrepentant. It is this sort of thing that Christian theologian Albert Schweitzer had in mind when he said, "A quiet conscience is the invention of the Devil." Or, in our case, the invention of Mara.

. . .

A more sensitive form of the argument from mindfulness is made by Sister Chan Khong. "If we [eat mindfully], we may find that our appetite for meat and fish begins to diminish. The important thing is to be aware of what we consume." Chan Khong has taken the vow of lifelong vegetarianism that Nhat Hanh administers to all those whom he ordains as monks or nuns.[9] Since she, like Nhat Hanh himself, follows a compassionate vegetarian diet, her argument is not self-serving; she is speaking from conviction.

Even so, it is not a persuasive argument, because it implies that being aware that we are doing harm and causing suffering to sentient beings is more important than actually not doing harm and causing suffering. The cows, pigs, and chickens of the world would not agree. And for that reason, I would suggest that being aware of what we consume is not "the important thing" about our eating, it is the important *first step* toward a compassionate diet. If awareness of the suffering and death that suffuses our food does not motivate us to eat as harmlessly as possible, than our mindfulness is incomplete. If we are fully and genuinely mindful in our eating, we will not allow our choice of foods to bring needless suffering and death to living beings.

In fact, being mindful of the suffering and death that suffuses every piece of meat and choosing to eat the meat anyway can be worse than not being mindful at all. We know better and we do it anyway. For the sake of pleasure, we stifle our compassion. This is why the Buddha said, "One who takes flesh kills the seed of great compassion."[10]

The hardest thing for many Western Buddhists to understand about a compassionate diet is that *it's not about us, it's about the animals.* Buddhist compassion is first and foremost about relieving the suffering of sentient beings, not promoting our own spiritual growth or sense of virtue and well-being. The Buddha had reached the acme of spiritual growth; he had progressed beyond karma; nothing he could do would be of any spiritual benefit to him because he was already a perfectly developed spiritual being. But instead of reaping the benefits by passing immediately into nirvana, he chose to spend the remaining 45 years of his life here in samsara, "for the good of the many, for the happiness of the many, out of compassion for the world." The Buddha's compassion was not about his own spiritual well-being, it was about the suffering of living beings.

Compassion for our own sake isn't compassion at all; it's self-love and attachment wearing the disguise of compassion. In *The Compassionate Life*, the Dalai Lama quotes with approval the great Tibetan teacher Je Tsongkhapa (1357–1419): "The more the practitioner engages in activities and thoughts that are focused and directed toward the fulfillment of others' well-being, the fulfillment or realization of his or her own aspiration will come as a byproduct without having to make a separate effort."[11]

There are two important points here. First, a Buddhist practitioner should engage in "*activities* and thoughts . . . directed toward the fulfillment of others' well-being." It is not enough to hold compassionate thoughts in our minds; our actions must be equally compassionate and directed toward the welfare of other living beings. Our behavior must reflect our mental attitude. Second, the "realization of [our] own aspiration" is not the purpose of Buddhist mindfulness and compassion; it is a "byproduct." When our mindfulness is compassionate—primarily for the benefit of other sentient beings—our own benefit comes about naturally. When our mindfulness is selfish—primarily for our own benefit—no one is the better for it.

Kate Lawrence has the focus exactly right when she says, "When we bring mindfulness to the dinner table, it suffuses the rest of our lives as well. . . . If consumers eliminate meat consumption entirely, the operation of slaughterhouses—and all the suffering and devastation of meat production and consumption—can be permanently brought to an end."[12]

When we hunt or fish, we deliberately kill a defenseless being who wishes us no harm. This is a direct violation of the First Precept. It is absolutely forbidden to Buddhists. As to eating meat, we know that the only way we can obtain it is for an animal to be killed. Therefore, when we eat meat, it is our intent that an innocent animal should die to satisfy our addiction to flesh. And that underlying intention—no matter how well hidden behind a smokescreen of rationalizations—will block the growth of compassion and create negative karma.

One of my grandmother's favorite sayings was "Beauty is as beauty does." Buddhism teaches us that "Compassion is as compassion does." Mahathera Saddhatissa, whom we quoted earlier, told us that "A Buddhist does not sacrifice living beings for worship or food, but sacrifices instead his own selfish motives."[13]

The Argument from Attachment

The Buddha taught that all desires for things that we think will bring us happiness in samsara are addictions, no different psychologically from alcoholism or drug addiction. Many Buddhist spiritual exercises are designed to help us break free of our addictions—which in Buddhist terminology are known collectively as "attachment" or "clinging"—because they are what bind us to suffering. There is no way to reach nirvana except by freeing ourselves from them.

Buddhist meat-eaters sometimes defend their diet by claiming that "dogmatic insistence" on a vegetarian or vegan lifestyle is a form of clinging that is contrary to the spirit of Buddhism. Buddhist practitioners, they suggest, should be able to take meat or leave it alone and not make a fetish of their diet.

If a Buddhist vegan diet were undertaken for the benefit of the practitioner, there might be some merit in this claim. But it is not. A Buddhist vegan diet is undertaken out of compassion for the suffering of animals. Every morsel of meat that we eat, every slice of cheese, every omelet comes at the price of cruel, unnatural confinement and childhood death. We cannot eat animal products even occasionally without supporting the torture and killing of innocent animals. Every retreat from

veganism toward "moderation" or a "middle way" is a step farther into cruelty and killing.

The Buddha never advocated a "middle way" between
good and evil or compassion and cruelty. And he most certainly never taught that we should strive to conquer our
"attachment" to compassion. In fact, he taught that we should
do everything in our power to strengthen our compassion. A
vegan lifestyle is an expression of compassion, it is not a form
of clinging to the addictions of samsara. The attachment that
meat-eating Buddhists should be concerned about is their
craving for the flesh of murdered animals, not the determination to live a life based on ahimsa.

One last point, or rather one more repetition of my endless
theme: If insistence on a lifestyle that does not depend on the
murder of animals is a form of clinging, what about insistence
on a lifestyle that does not depend on the murder of human
beings? Is that also a form of clinging? If so, does that mean
we should be able to take or leave armed robbery and murder?
And if not, what is the difference other than the species of the
victim? The argument from attachment is simply speciesism
dressed up in Buddhist language.

Ye Olde Karmic Connection

Perhaps the most arrogant of the mind games that Buddhist
meat-eaters play is the argument from the karmic connection.
"When we kill an animal," this argument runs, "or eat the
flesh of an animal, we establish a karmic connection. And
because of that bond, the animal will enjoy a favorable rebirth
and will eventually become a dharma practitioner and attain
enlightenment. Therefore, we are actually helping the animal
by eating him."

The seed from which this self-serving fantasy grew is the
Buddhist teaching that contact with a Buddha, bodhisattva, or

arhat establishes a karmic connection with that holy being which will ultimately work to your advantage. Harming a Buddha, for example, is one of the "sins of immediate retribution," leading to rebirth in the hell realms. But because of your karmic connection with the Buddha, as soon as you have exhausted the negative karma that sent you there, you will be reborn in circumstances favorable to practicing dharma and progressing toward enlightenment. Unfortunately, the karmic connection only works with holy beings who are not themselves subject to karma. And that is why I called this argument "arrogant." It presumes that the average, everyday Buddhist meat-eater, including the person making the argument, is a holy being, a dubious proposition to say the least.

Nowhere in the sutras or the teachings of the ancient sages do we find the notion that animals killed for food by ordinary beings benefit karmically from their misfortune. What we do find is the warning that those who participate—even indirectly—in the killing of innocent animals will suffer in future lives because of the negative karma they incur. People who like to start their day with bacon and eggs, for example, may well find themselves reborn as pigs confined on a factory farm from the day they are born until the day they are sent to the slaughterhouse—or hens in a battery cage with no sunlight, no fresh air, and no room even to turn around or spread their wings.

The Arguments from Perfection

In the modern world—probably in any of the visible realms—it is impossible to be a perfect vegan. Absolute ahimsa is beyond our grasp. Thich Nhat Hanh reminds us that "Even if we take pride in being vegetarian, for example, we have to acknowledge that the water in which we boil our vegetables contains many tiny microorganisms."[14] I think it is extremely doubtful that microorganisms are sentient beings, but putting that aside, there is no way to feed a human population without some loss of animal life. Plant agriculture on any sizable scale always involves some level of killing, be it worms and grubs, insects, field mice and other small animals, or ground nesting birds. Some Buddhists argue that since fruit and vegetable production require the killing of animals, there is no reason not to kill a few more animals for meat. This is an argument that depends on telling only part of the story.

Animal agriculture kills far more animals than the 48 billion who die every year in the world's slaughterhouses. According to David Pimentel, a professor of agricultural science at Cornell University, and Henry Kendall, a Nobel prize-winning physicist, "about 38 percent of the world's grain goes to feed livestock."[15] In the United States, which has one of the world's most meat-intensive diets, the percentage is probably much higher. Furthermore, turning animals into nutrient processing systems is a very inefficient way to produce food. *American Agriculturist*, a trade journal, estimates that on average it takes more than 10 pounds of grain to produce one pound of beef.[16] If the world adopted a vegan diet, we would be able to drastically reduce the amount of grain, soybeans, and corn that we raise without sacrificing human nutrition. This, in turn, would sharply reduce the number of small animals, birds, and insects killed in plant agriculture.

. . .

From a Buddhist perspective, there is an ethical and karmic distinction between deliberately killing living beings, as in animal agriculture, and inadvertently killing living beings, as happens in plant agriculture. It is true that large-scale monocrop agriculture involves the deliberate killing of insects and worms through the use of pesticides, but the growing of grain, corn, and soybeans for livestock also involves the use of these toxic chemicals.

There is also the further distinction to be made between animal agriculture, which is not essential for human life, and plant agriculture, which is. Minimal killing in the course of an activity essential to human life may not be virtuous, but it is much less wrong than killing in the course of an activity that is not essential to human life. This is why animal husbandry is forbidden to Buddhists as contrary to right livelihood, while plant farming is not.

The impossibility of feeding a human population without causing some level of death in the animal realm is a tragedy that is built into the structure of samsara; there is nothing that we can do about it. Thich Nhat Hanh tells us, "We cannot be completely nonviolent, but by being vegetarian, we are going in the direction of nonviolence."[17] And this is precisely the point. Our challenge is to reduce the pain and death that we cause to the absolute minimum. *We must resist the temptation to let the harm that we will inevitably do become an excuse for avoidable harm inflicted for the sake of appetite, habit, or convenience.* It is impossible to eliminate fatal accidents from America's highways. But no one would suggest that this justifies deliberately running down pedestrians. In the same way, the fact that some animals are necessarily killed in plant agriculture does not justify the unnecessary killing of other animals for their flesh.

As I remarked earlier, a truly Buddhist society would grow its food on small organic farms that distribute locally, since that would require the least loss of life. This, in turn, would require a considerable scaling down of our cities and a significant reduction in the human population—both of which would be a good thing for a lot of reasons. But we do not live in this ideal Buddhist society, and none of us is going to in this lifetime. The challenge of Buddhist ethics is to live in an imperfect world as closely to perfection as we are able. We succeed by not giving in to the temptation to use the impossibility of perfection as an excuse for laziness in our practice of compassion.

CHAPTER 12

THE WESTERN SEDUCTION

Joseph Goldstein and Lama Surya Das are two of the most popular Western teachers of Buddhism. Before we examine their teachings on eating meat, I want to make it clear that I am not singling them out because their teachings on animals are more egregious than those of other Western teachers. Quite the opposite, I have chosen them because of the clarity with which they express two of the most common approaches in Western Buddhism to the eating of meat.

Joseph Goldstein is a highly respected teacher of insight meditation (Pali, *vipassana;* Sanskrit, *vipashyana*), and rightly so. His books *The Experience of Insight* and *Insight Meditation* are beautifully written, profound, and accessible to the Western reader while remaining faithful to the original teachings. After extensive study with Burmese and Indian meditation masters who taught in the Theravada tradition, Goldstein studied with Tibetan lamas, and his most recent book, *One Dharma*, proposes that Western Buddhism build upon the essential unity of all Buddhist traditions without getting enmeshed in sectarianism and labeling.

In *One Dharma*, Goldstein synopsizes the fundamental principles of Buddhism by quoting the Buddha: "Do no harm, act for the good, purify the mind." He recognizes that the first element of this triad raises questions about the permissibility of eating meat. But he disposes of them in the cursory manner of someone getting the bothersome trivia quickly out of the way so that he can move on to the important stuff. His entire discussion of our treatment of animals takes up only two paragraphs, less than one page in a book with 194 pages of text. Goldstein's conclusion: "There is no one right answer to this question of diet. Our task is to stay awake to our own sensibilities, to be willing to investigate different courses of action, to not hold the taking of life lightly, and with whatever we do to maintain a heart of compassion."[1]

"There is no one right answer" because Goldstein is asking the wrong question. And he is asking the wrong question because he is looking in the wrong direction. He is looking at the perpetrators and not the victims; he is looking at Buddhist practitioners when he should be looking at the animals they eat. *It's not about us. It's about the animals.* Eating meat is not about "our diet," it is about the killing of 48 billion sentient beings every year. Compassion is not about the "sensibilities" of the practitioner, it is about the suffering and death of sentient beings. Despite Goldstein's soothing phrase, it is not possible to "maintain a heart of compassion" while you condone and support the killing of sentient beings to indulge a craving for food that you don't need in order to be healthy. And to think that you can is self-deception. This is why the *Brahmajala Sutra* quotes the Buddha as saying that "Anyone who eats flesh is cutting himself off from the great seed of his own merciful and compassionate nature."[2]

Despite the platitudes that follow about not taking killing "lightly" and maintaining "a heart of compassion," the statement that "our task is to stay awake to our own sensibilities" constitutes a moral abdication where nonhuman sentient beings are concerned. The function of Buddhist ethical teachings is to steer our sensibilities toward the welfare of others, not follow them into cruelty for the sake of our own pleasure. The correct question is not, "Should I be a vegetarian?" but "Should I participate in the unnecessary killing of sentient beings?" This shifts the focus from practitioner to victim. The first question is all about "me," and slides delicately past the horrendous effects that my self-absorption have on other sentient beings. When we recast the issue in terms of compassion, it becomes immediately clear that Buddhist teaching—as well as simple human decency—does in fact prescribe "one right answer to this question of diet."

. . .

As an example of a morally acceptable approach to eating meat, Goldstein says, "Or, as in many native cultures, people may accept the larger cycles of birth and death in nature and act from that understanding with compassion and responsibility."[3] This is a distressingly common theme in American Buddhism, one that overlooks the fact that the intensive confinement farms and conveyer-belt slaughterhouses that produce America's meat bear no relationship to the animal husbandry practices of native cultures. No native society would force hens to spend their entire lives crammed into battery cages so small that they cannot turn around or spread their wings, where there is no natural sunlight or fresh air and the stench of ammonia from their urine is so thick that workers have to wear masks to enter the building. No native society would force sows to spend their entire adult lives lying on a hard concrete floor in a farrowing pen so small they cannot stand up. And no native society would take a calf from his mother when he is only a day or two old, imprison him in a cell so narrow that he cannot lie down or turn around, feed him a diet so deficient in iron that he becomes severely anemic, and then kill him while he is still a child simply because people enjoy the texture of veal. The invocation of native cultures to defend modern meat-eating is specious.

As the Dalai Lama pointed out in his proclamation on hunting, in Buddhism, nothing is more important than compassion, and culture is never an excuse for cruelty, whether it is the hunting rituals of Native Americans or the fried chicken for Sunday dinner that was traditional in my Southern Baptist family when I was a child. We Western Buddhists should be teaching our own culture to live without cruelty and killing, not casting about in other cultures for excuses to cling to our addictions.

The interesting thing about "these larger cycles of birth and death in nature" is that human beings are almost always the killers and rarely the killed. And when one of us does happen to be killed by an animal (usually because of our own carelessness or stupidity), we regard it as an outrage, a violation of the natural order of things. This reaction would strongly suggest that if we were regularly the prey instead of the predator, we might not feel quite so in harmony with "these larger cycles." A compassionate spirit always regards the opinion of the oppressed as more valid than the opinion of the oppressor.

Eat, Drink, and Be Merry
Like Joseph Goldstein, Lama Surya Das (Jeffrey Miller) is a highly respected and extremely popular Buddhist teacher.

Certified by a Tibetan abbot, he is fully entitled to call himself "Lama," a claim that not many Westerners can make. A charismatic teacher, Surya Das has a wide following in the United States, and his extremely well-written books, especially *Awakening the Buddhist Heart* and *Awakening the Buddha Within*, make the often recondite doctrines of Tibetan Buddhism readily accessible to Western spiritual seekers.

Surya Das contributes a column to Beliefnet, a popular website and online subscription service dealing with religion. Asked the question, "Do you have to give up meat, alcohol, and sex to be a good Buddhist?" his answer was, "Not at all." He went on to explain that Buddhism stresses "ethical morality, meditative awareness, and wisdom, coupled with love and unselfishness. So meat, alcohol, and sex are not the top evils for Buddhists."[4] After saying that vegetarianism "makes good sense as a way to practice nonviolence and lovingkindness as well as gain health benefits," Surya Das is at pains to point out that "there are plenty of meat-eating Buddhists in both Asia and the West."[5]

Ignoring the fact that "right view" is the first step on the Noble Eightfold Path, Surya Das goes on to say that "Buddhism is not about beliefs, but about practices. . . . One can be a genuine Buddhist without necessarily subscribing to . . . any particular belief, including vegetarianism, reincarnation, or the existence of other worlds and lives."[6] But, as Surya Das himself acknowledged when he called it "a way to practice nonviolence and lovingkindness," vegetarianism is not a belief, it is a practice. Therefore, even by his definition, vegetarianism is precisely the sort of thing that Buddhism is about. Like Joseph Goldstein, Surya Das is looking the wrong way. When he calls vegetarianism a "belief," he is looking at the practitioner and ignoring the suffering of the animals.

In common with all too many Western teachers, Lama

Surya Das seems willing to make optional anything in Buddhism that might make a Western practitioner uncomfortable. Are you addicted to Big Macs? Do you like to toss back a few cold ones while you're watching the game? Do you hope you get lucky when you hit the singles bars on Saturday night? No problem. "Meat, alcohol, and sex are not the top evils for Buddhists." In one stroke, he has cancelled two of the Five Precepts.[7] Thich Nhat Hanh reminds us that, "When we buy something or consume something, we may be participating in an act of killing. [The first] precept reflects our determination not to kill, either directly or indirectly, and to prevent others from killing."[8] And so, the First Precept prohibits meat-eating. The Fifth Precept forbids the drinking of alcohol or the non-medical use of drugs that affect the mind. It does not, as Surya Das suggests, "proscribe" only "the misuse of alcohol."[9]

Most of the beliefs and practices that Surya Das is willing to declare optional are, in fact, less important than the practices he stresses—mindfulness, lovingkindness, compassion, and wisdom. He is exactly right: These are the heart of Buddhism. Whether we have a glass of wine with dinner or have sex without being married is less important than whether we are mindful, loving, kind, and compassionate. But he fails to recognize that meat-eating is in an altogether different category than sex and alcohol because it is inherently devoid of mercy.[10]

. . .

I think that Joseph Goldstein's and Surya Das's permissive attitude about meat-eating reflects the values that most of their students bring to Buddhism. Americans attracted to Buddhism tend to fit the same broad profile.[11] We were raised Jewish or Christian and first came to Buddhism between our mid-twenties and mid-forties; we are white, middle-class, college educated, often with graduate degrees, work in professional or managerial careers, and, unless we have deliberately "returned to the land," we dwell in the cities and suburbs. The intellectual orientation of most of us is the liberal humanism that became the dominant social outlook of the democratic West during the era of the baby boom generation.

Our core value is comfort. We seek that which creates comfort, be it spiritual, intellectual, emotional, physical, or economic. At the same time, we are generous, and we count making others uncomfortable among the most heinous of offenses. Our most deeply held commitment is to openness, tolerance, diversity, and respect for all points of view. We hold firmly to the belief that having firmly held beliefs is a sign of ignorance, provincialism, and stunted spiritual growth. We came to Buddhism seeking spiritual and emotional comfort, and we are loath to define Buddhism in any way that makes ourselves or others uncomfortable.

To many Western spiritual seekers, ethical veganism can look like just another intolerant, self-righteous dogma: "I am holier than thou because I don't eat meat." We chose Buddhism in large part because we were fed up with the dogmas of Christianity and Judaism, and we are not about to adopt a new set. That is why *it is vital to take the focus off the practitioner and put it onto the animals who suffer and die in the production of our food.* There is no other way to overcome the resistance of most Western Buddhists. *It's not about us; it's about the animals.* A vegan lifestyle is not a dogma, it is an essential element of Buddhist compassion. And vegans are intolerant of meat-eating only in the way that we are all intolerant of the murder of humans.

Dissonant Dharma

This characteristically Western focus on the practitioner to the exclusion of other sentient beings is epitomized by composer Philip Glass, who serves on the Board of Directors of *Tricycle* magazine. A vegetarian for nearly three decades, Glass denies the validity of compassion as a reason to adopt a vegetarian diet:

> The question of compassion can be tricky also. After all, sentient beings are going to die anyway, and perhaps some of those deaths will serve the needs of others, proving to be beneficial in their way (or so the argument goes). Not to mention that I have yet to meet a Tibetan lama from the lowest rank to the highest who is a vegetarian.[12]

The parenthetical disclaimer seems intended to distance Glass from his own argument, suggesting that at some level he understands how silly it is and raising the question of why he brought it up in the first place. We are all "going to die anyway," and this line of reasoning could be used to justify the killing of anyone whose death might benefit others. It would, for example, justify the use of unwilling or uninformed human beings as subjects in biomedical experiments, not to mention the dispatching of aged relatives whose heirs would benefit from their estates.

Glass then proceeds to the argument for vegetarianism that he finds most persuasive:

> In vegetarianism as practice we view all sentient beings—fish, birds, cows, bugs, etc.—as equal to ourselves. This becomes a practice to develop equanimity to *all* sentient beings (even the delicious ones). . . . Put simply, equanimity is a powerful opponent of the self-cherishing and self-grasping that are at the root cause of

ignorance. . . . Viewed in this way . . . vegetarianism is proposed not on moral or ethical grounds (i.e., "you shouldn't eat meat because it is wrong"), but as a potentially powerful tool for our own spiritual development.[13]

As my wife, Patti Rogers, often says, "The animals don't care *why* you don't eat them, only *that* you don't." And she is right. I am glad that Philip Glass is a vegetarian for whatever reason. But, allowing that, Glass's argument raises four concerns: First, since Buddhists are free to choose from among many skillful means for training their minds, Glass's vegetarianism is optional; Buddhists are free to adopt it or not, according to their own inclination. This provides no incentive toward the creation of a vegan world in which no animals will suffer on factory farms or die in slaughterhouses, and to that extent at the very least, it represents a failure of compassion.

Second, by uncoupling vegetarianism from morality and ethics, Glass denies the teachings of the Buddha in both the Pali Canon and the Mahayana sutras that our treatment of animals is an ethical issue of the first order. And by doing so, it treats the suffering and death of animals, "beings like us," as of no consequence.

Third, by insisting on seeing morality and ethics as a set of rules imposed for the sake of controlling someone else's behavior by guilt, Glass fails to recognize the true nature of Buddhist ethics as essential expressions of Buddhist compassion.

Finally, Buddhist practice divorced from ethics is a kind of spiritual narcissism, and as such it strengthens the ego rather than helping us to overcome it. Therefore, even on Glass's terms, it fails as Buddhist practice. In this regard, I am reminded of T. S. Eliot's observation in *Murder in the Cathedral* that "the greatest treason" is "to do the right deed for the wrong reason."

Paralytic Buddhism

Roshi Robert Aitken is an eloquent advocate of engaged Buddhism. Although a vegetarian, Aitken eats meat when attending dinner parties where meat is served because, "The cow is dead and the hostess is not."[14] When we eat meat to avoid embarrassing our hostess, we lend our approval to the slaughter of animals for food. Whether we intend to or not, we tell everyone in attendance that we believe eating meat is an ethically acceptable practice for Buddhists. And in so doing, we lose a unique opportunity to spread the Buddha's message of nonviolence toward all living beings without exception.

An extreme example of this tendency to relate to both sides of an issue so thoroughly that the moral core of the Buddhadharma vanishes in a blur of conflicting perspectives appeared in a recent issue of *Turning Wheel*, the journal of the Buddhist Peace Fellowship.

Trena Cleland, a member of a Buddhist group that provides meals to homeless shelters, states with uncommon straightforwardness a viewpoint that is common among Western Buddhists. "One aspect of Buddhism that I find very challenging is the teaching that no point of view can be declared absolutely right or wrong, good or bad, true or false. The dharma warns that attachment to what we 'know' leads to suffering, and encourages us to honor life's gray areas rather than hold fast to judgments and opinions."[15]

As in the case of the argument from emptiness, this interpretation of Buddhism's teaching on judgments and opinions commits the category mistake of confusing the ultimate with the relative. The fact that "no point of view can be declared absolutely right or wrong" does not mean that points of view cannot be declared relatively right or wrong depending on how well they facilitate our practice of compassion and our approach to wisdom. As long as we live in the world of relative truth, we must act in the world of relative truth, and the refusal to make relative judgments leads to a paralysis that can quickly become complicit with evil.

The dharma teaches us to regard all judgments and opinions as provisional, to hold fast to them as long as and to the extent that they help us proceed toward the development of the great compassion and the great wisdom, and then, when they have served their purpose, to transcend them. The notion that all points of view are valid and should be respected is not a Buddhist teaching. It is the view of Western liberal humanism. The Buddhist teaching is that some views and activities constitute skillful means for practicing compassion and gaining wisdom and others do not. And we are to hold to the former and let go of the latter. As my teacher, Lama Kalsang, taught me, "The essence of the Buddhadharma is learning what to hold on to and what to let go of." But we do have to let go. To hold on to everything is to hold on to nothing.

The Buddha did not hesitate to call certain actions "virtuous" and others "evil," a point that is often lost on his modern-day followers. Universal compassion does not mean acceding to every point of view that we are presented with. It means making the most informed and unbiased decision that we can as to what is the most compassionate thing to do in any given situation—and then doing it. Moral paralysis defeats even the most compassionate of intentions.

Ms. Cleland and her group were serving vegetarian meals to the residents of a homeless shelter. One of the men being fed claimed that giving them only vegetarian food was a form of oppression and injustice. He compared the shelter volunteers to missionaries who disrespected indigenous cultures and forced their way of life on unwilling peoples. "You don't give us what we want—you give us what you think we should have," he told them.[16] This charge threw the group into a tizzy, and when the article was published the issue of whether to serve meat or vegetarian food at shelters had still not been resolved.

Animals have a vital interest in not suffering on factory farms and being killed in slaughterhouses. The people in the shelter had a much lesser interest in being served the type of food they preferred. Even their interest in being able to exercise some small degree of control over their lives was less important than the interests of the animals. After all, a pig being prodded down the chute to slaughter has no control over his life, either. The volunteers at the shelter saw the plight and heard the complaints of the residents first hand. Before reaching a decision, I hope they will tour a slaughterhouse and see the plight and hear the screams of the animals.

THE DIAMOND VEHICLE
AND THE DALAI LAMA

I think it is safe to say that along with Hinduism and Jainism—its fellow ahimsa-based Indian religions—Buddhism has the highest proportion of vegetarians of any major religion. There are no accurate statistics, but I would guess—and it is only a guess—that worldwide about half of all Buddhists are vegetarian.[1] Chinese Buddhism (including Chan and Pure Land) boasts the highest proportion of vegetarians, probably followed by Theravada and Zen. There is no question that the highest proportion of meat-eaters is found in Tibetan Buddhism, which is why it merits its own chapter.

When asked about their diet, Tibetans rarely try to defend meat-eating on religious grounds. Instead, they point out that climate and soil conditions over much of the Tibetan plateau do not permit plant agriculture on a scale that would support the human population. When Tibet converted to Buddhism, they say, the people continued to eat meat out of necessity.

Whether we accept that or not, it fails to address the fact that most Tibetans—including lamas—who live in India,

Nepal, and the West have continued to eat meat. I once asked His Holiness Sakya Trizin, the head of the Sakyapa, one of the four main denominations of Tibetan Buddhism, why this is so, and he answered this way. "It is a habit ingrained in our culture for thousands of years. We should be vegetarians, but we find it too hard to break the habit. In compassion for living beings in the animal realm, vegetarians are better Buddhist practitioners than people who eat meat. Vegetarianism is a higher form of Buddhist practice."

I am not unsympathetic to the problem. But much of Buddhist practice is directed at breaking the force of bad habits and teaching us to control our cravings, including cravings that are culturally inculcated. I have large areas in my own life where I have failed to accomplish that, and so I am not presuming to sit in judgment of those who, although still human, are far more highly advanced than I. Every Tibetan teacher I have known is a kind and compassionate Buddhist practitioner, and none more so than His Holiness Sakya Trizin. But this does not change the fact that meat-eating violates Buddhist principles of ahimsa and compassion no matter who engages in it. I am confident that someday soon the compassion of these great teachers will lead them to adopt a vegan diet for the benefit of living beings.

. . .

In one sense, I agree with His Holiness's statement that "vegetarianism is a higher form of Buddhist practice." But in another sense, I believe he had it exactly backwards. As long as we regard vegetarianism as a "higher" form of practice to be pursued only by those who are unusually compassionate or diligent, we excuse meat-eating by everyone else. Veganism is simply letting compassion guide our choice of food. As such, it is a basic Buddhist practice that ought to be expected of everyone who takes refuge vows.

. . .

Nevertheless, Tibetan Buddhism has a far stronger tradition of compassionate animal protection and vegetarianism than most people realize.

Jigme Lingpa (1729–1798) is revered as a highly realized practitioner of the most advanced practices of Tibetan Buddhism. His biographer, Janet Gyatso, says that, "Of all his merit-making, Jigme Lingpa was most proud of his feelings of compassion for animals."[2] She tells of "his sorrow . . . when he witnessed the butchering of animals by humans. He often bought and set free animals about to be slaughtered (a common Buddhist act).[3] He 'changed the perception' of others, such as his Pala sponsors, whom he once caused to save a female yak from being butchered, and he continually urged his disciples to forswear the killing of animals. When he learned of an extensive massacre of bees for honey on a particular mountain, he bought the entire mountain and 'sealed' it off from hunting 'until the end of the eon.' "[4] Shabkar Tsogdruk Rangdrol (1781–1851) was one of the most beloved teachers in the history of Tibet. A pioneer of the rime movement, Shabkar was a vegetarian for most of his adult life. In his autobiography, he tells us why. "I saw many sheep and goats that had been slaughtered. Feeling unbearable compassion for all animals in the world who are killed for food, I went back before the Jowo Rinpoche, prostrated myself, and made this vow: 'From today on, I give up the negative act that is eating the flesh of beings, each one of whom has been my mother.' "[5] Shabkar frequently took part in the practice of animal liberation, and insisted that all slaughter of animals stop.

"Above all," he told meat-eaters, "all beings have been our parents in previous lives; therefore, it is utterly wrong to kill in order to obtain the worst of all foods: the flesh and blood of living beings."[6] On a trip to Nepal, he persuaded so many professional hunters that their way of life was contrary to the Buddhadharma that meat merchants complained he was ruining their business.[7]

There could be no more heartfelt condemnation of meat-eating than this passage by Patrul Rinpoche (1808–1887), one of the most respected teachers of the nineteenth century. "In Buddhism, once we have taken refuge in the dharma we have to give up harming others. To have an animal killed everywhere we go, and to enjoy its flesh and blood, is surely against the precepts of taking refuge, is it not? More particularly, in the Bodhisattva tradition of the Great Vehicle [Mahayana Buddhism], we are supposed to be the refuge and protector of all infinite beings [all living beings without exception]. The beings with unfortunate karma that we are supposed to be protecting are instead being killed without the slightest compassion, and their boiled flesh and blood are being presented to us, and we—their protectors, the Bodhisattvas—then gobble it all up gleefully, smacking our lips. What could be worse than that?"[8]

Today, there is an active and growing vegetarian movement within Tibetan Buddhism, spearheaded by the Universal Compassion Movement (UCM), founded and led by a Buddhist monk, Geshe Thupten Phelgye. Headquartered in Dharamsala, India, the Dalai Lama's home in exile, UCM actively promotes vegetarianism and a variety of relief projects for both animals and humans.

The Diamond Vehicle
Tibetan Buddhism is unique among contemporary Buddhist

schools for its practice of the *Vajrayana* ("Diamond Vehicle"), a set of esoteric techniques intended to help the practitioner develop bodhichitta more quickly than is possible by more conventional means. A subset of the Mahayana, the Vajrayana developed in India around 500 CE and spread to Tibet 300 years later.[9] It differs from other forms of Buddhism in that, rather than trying to eradicate unwholesome states of mind and then replace them with wholesome attitudes, it professes to transform those unwholesome states directly into purified states. Most Buddhist schools regard unwholesome thoughts as troublesome things to be gotten rid of; the Vajrayana regards them as raw material for the creation of bodhichitta. It is a kind of spiritual alchemy that transmutes the lead of sins and obscurations into the gold of enlightenment.

This approach has led some practitioners to regard Vajrayana practice as a free pass to indulge in immoral behavior without suffering the karmic consequences or impeding their spiritual progress. "If unwholesome activities are the raw material of enlightenment," they say, "then we should feel free to indulge in them. All that matters is that we do so with the correct mental attitude," whatever that may be. From the Indian master Padmasambhava, who first brought the Vajrayana to Tibet around 800 CE, down to the present, the great teachers have condemned the corruption of the Vajrayana into an excuse for immoral behavior. Padmasambhava himself was unequivocal on this point. "In my Secret Mantra [Vajrayana] teachings, the profound view is most important, but it is absolutely necessary to behave well, in addition."[10] The goal of the Vajrayana is bodhichitta. It was never meant to be a rationale for denying our compassion to suffering beings.

Some of the confusion arises because Buddhist legends portray various Vajrayana masters, both Indian and Tibetan, as behaving in ways that are perfectly outrageous if not down-right immoral. But they engaged in this kind of behavior only after they gained a high level of spiritual realization, not before, and so this behavior was actually a skillful means that did not harm other sentient beings despite appearances to the contrary. As highly realized beings, they had the power to manifest illusory appearances so that their extreme behavior harmed no living being and could not retard their own spiritual progress. In the Tibetan tradition, these masters are said to possess "crazy wisdom."

An example of a "crazy yogi" is the ancient Indian *mahasiddha*, or Vajrayana master, Virupa, who was fired from his teaching post at a Buddhist university because officials believed they had seen him partying in his bedroom with several young women in varying stages of undress. But in fact, what appeared to be attractive young women were actually dakinis, spiritual beings who were imparting Buddhist teachings to Virupa.[11]

As this anecdote should make clear, stories of Vajrayana masters behaving in a decidedly unspiritual fashion are intended to illustrate the power of Vajrayana meditation, not to serve as excuses for those who us who are prone to indulge our less spiritual cravings. Since most of us do not possess these spiritual powers, we cannot—and should not—model our behavior after the conduct of these mahasiddhas. And we certainly should not use the Vajrayana as an excuse for not showing compassion to sentient beings.

The proper relationship of the Vajrayana to other Buddhist teachings is expressed in a formula that is widely taught in Tibetan Buddhism: "Let your behavior be according to the Hinayana [strictly in accord with the Five Precepts]. Let your motivation be according to the Mahayana [to gain enlightenment for the benefit of all living beings]. And let your meditation be according to the Vajrayana [guided visualizations and other esoteric techniques]."[12] From this perspective, these three approaches to Buddhism are complementary, not contradictory. They are three strands in a single cord, woven seamlessly together.

· · ·

That the Vajrayana does not relieve the practitioner of the obligation to ease the suffering of living beings is made clear from the story of Avalokiteshvara (Tibetan: Chenrezig), the bodhisattva of compassion, and an extremely popular meditational deity (*yidam*) in Vajrayana Buddhism. Many ages ago, Avalokiteshvara was so moved by compassion for the suffering of living beings that he made a vow not to rest until he had relieved the suffering of them all, sealing the vow with the wish that if his resolve should fail, his body might shatter into a thousand pieces. After eons of tireless effort, Avalokiteshvara paused to look around and see how much progress he had made. Seeing that beings beyond number were still mired in suffering, he grew discouraged and gave up his effort. Immediately, his body shattered into a thousand pieces. Taking pity on him, Amitabha, the Buddha of Boundless Light, collected the pieces and put Avalokiteshvara back together, but with one difference: The reassembled bodhisattva had a thousand arms, one for each of the pieces into which his body had broken, the better to be able to help living beings.[13]

In our context, the point of the story is that authentic compassion inspires us to work tirelessly for the benefit of living beings, not complacently ignore their suffering—much less continue to cause it. Avalokiteshvara had achieved bodhichitta; he could have rested eternally in the undisturbed bliss of nirvana. But he did not. He was compelled by the great compas-

sion to spend countless eons of unrelenting effort freeing living beings from suffering, a labor we are told that he pursues
to this day. If the great Vajrayana yidam, Avalokiteshvara, was
moved by an overwhelming need to put his compassion to
work relieving the suffering of living beings, it seems clear that
Vajrayana practitioners should feel a similar obligation.

Along with Avalokiteshvara, Tara (Tibetan: Drolma) is the
most frequently encountered and best loved yidam in
Vajrayana Buddhism. Tara represents the compassionate activity of all the Buddhas. It is to Tara, "the Great Mother, the
Wish-Fulfilling Wheel," that Tibetan Buddhists most often
pray when they are in trouble or need help. The existence of
an important Vajrayana yidam who is specifically devoted to
alleviating the suffering of sentient beings while they remain
in samsara is proof that Vajrayana compassion should be
active in the world, not confined to meditational practices or
limited to helping living beings attain enlightenment. Traditionally, Tara practices are done early in the morning, and for
the remainder of the day the practitioner is encouraged to
maintain a vegetarian diet, a striking example of vegetarianism as an expression of Vajrayana Buddhist compassion.[14]

In Chinese and Japanese Buddhism, it is Avalokiteshvara,
in female form and known as Kuan Yin (Japanese: Kanzeon,
Kannon), who most often answers prayers for help and eases
the suffering of sentient beings in samsara. Again, she is proof
that Buddhist compassion should be active in the world, and
not confined to meditational practices or limited to helping
living beings attain enlightenment.

His Holiness the Dalai Lama

When I talk to Buddhists about a vegan lifestyle, the two arguments I hear most often are, "The Buddha ate meat"—which
he did not—and "The Dalai Lama eats meat"—which he does.

In the Western press, Tenzin Gyatso, the Fourteenth Dalai Lama, is often referred to as "Tibet's god-king," but this is a misnomer. He is a bodhisattva, a spiritual hero who passes up the eternal joy of nirvana to keep returning to the troubles of samsara in order to ease the suffering of living beings. Additionally, the Dalai Lama is an "emanation" of Avalokiteshvara, which is to say that he embodies Avalokiteshvara's essence: compassion. This leads many Westerners—who grew up hearing that Jesus was without sin and the Pope is infallible—to believe that the Dalai Lama is infallible and cannot err. But this is not the Buddhist belief. When bodhisattvas and emanations take on human form, they also take on human nature. They have to struggle against the same temptations, weaknesses, and cravings that the rest of us do. It is part of the burden they willingly accept out of great compassion for living beings. Their many lifetimes of spiritual practice and their high level of realization gained during past lives equip them to overcome these obstacles far better than the rest of us, but they are not perfect. The fact that the Dalai Lama eats meat does not automatically mean that meat-eating is okay.

In fact, in the 1960s, moved by the sight of a chicken having her neck wrung so that he could eat her flesh for lunch, the Dalai Lama adopted a vegetarian diet. By this time, he had fled Tibet and was living in Dharamsala, India, where he should have had little trouble following a nutritious vegetarian regime. What foods His Holiness actually ate during his vegetarian period is not entirely clear, but he has said things to suggest that his staples may have been milk and nuts and that no real effort was made to balance his diet. However that may be, it was not long before he developed jaundice and had to be treated for hepatitis B.

Hepatitis B is a viral disease that is not caused by dietary deficiencies. Thanks to a vaccine developed in the 1980s, today it is relatively uncommon in the industrialized world, where, like AIDS, it is transmitted primarily by sexual contact or by sharing intravenous drug needles. In China, Tibet, and India in the 1960s, however, it was much more widespread and commonly transmitted by casual contact, including food prepared by someone who carried the virus. There is no way to know how the Dalai Lama contracted hepatitis B; he could have picked it up anywhere. What we do know, however, is that his vegetarian diet, no matter how poorly constructed, did not cause his hepatitis.

Be that as it may, the infection was successfully treated. But hepatitis B can cause cirrhosis of the liver, and the Dalai Lama's doctors—apparently both Tibetan and Western practitioners—told him that his liver had been affected and his life would probably be shortened as a result. It was imperative, they told him, that he resume eating meat for the sake of his health. And he did.

People with liver damage are often put on a high-protein diet, and in the 1960s, "high protein" and "meat" were synonymous in the minds of most health care professionals. Eventually, the Dalai Lama struck a compromise between his compassion and his doctors' orders. Now, he eats meat every other day, which means that he is vegetarian six months out of every year.

On November 10, 1998, Heidi Prescott, national director of The Fund for Animals, and I were granted a private audience with His Holiness specifically to discuss animal rights and vegetarianism. He told us the story I related in the preceding paragraphs,[15] and we appealed to him to seek further medical and nutritional advice with a view to adopting a vegetarian diet full time. We assured him that it is not difficult to maintain a balanced, nutritious diet high in protein without eating meat, and we recommended several sources of nutritional counseling, including the Physicians Committee for Responsible Medicine, well-known vegan physician Dr. Michael Klaper, and the Vegetarian Resource Group. Knowing His Holiness's remarkable compassion, I continue to pray that he will soon adopt a vegan diet. The Dalai Lama's example is a powerful influence on people around the world. His full-time adherence to a compassionate diet will save countless living beings from the slaughterhouse.

During our audience, His Holiness spoke movingly about the suffering of animals at the hands of humanity and expressed his strong support for activities on their behalf. "Whenever I visit a market," he told us, "and I see the chickens crowded together in tiny cages that give them no room to move around and spread their wings, and the fish slowly drowning in the air, my heart goes out to them. People have to learn to think about animals in a different way, as sentient beings who love life and fear death. I urge everyone who can adopt a compassionate vegetarian diet to do so." I asked if that meant he wanted to see more Buddhists and Tibetans become vegetarian. "Certainly," His Holiness replied. "In fact, I would like to see more vegetarian food in our monasteries and schools."

As the audience concluded, His Holiness bowed and pressed his hands together in front of his heart, fingers pointing upward, in the traditional Tibetan gesture of greeting and leave taking. "I thank all of you," he told us, "who are working to save animals from suffering. It is most important work."

· · ·

Although he is only a part-time vegetarian, the Dalai Lama is a full-time advocate for animal rights and a compassionate vegetarian diet.

One day I went to visit a small lake to offer food to the fish that we had previously freed there.[16] On my way back someone said, "By the way, did you see the poultry farm?" All of a sudden I had a vision of chickens carrying banners on which it was written, "The Dalai Lama not only saves fish, but even feeds them. What does he do for us poor chickens?" I felt terribly sad and sorry for the chickens. We no longer raise poultry in our settlements.[17]

In order to satisfy one human stomach, so many lives are taken away. We must promote vegetarianism. It is extremely important.[18]

· · ·

Every time I read in the press that the Dalai Lama has eaten steak in New York or lamb chops in San Diego, I cringe. "His Holiness Eats Meat" has become the new six-syllable mantra for meat-eating Buddhists. On a wider stage, the Dalai Lama may be the most universally respected moral leader in the world today. Buddhists and non-Buddhists alike who are looking for an excuse not to give up their daily fix of dead animal are all too eager to cite his meat-eating. In the winter of 2003, the Takoma Park–Silver Spring Co-op in the Maryland suburbs of Washington, D.C. announced a plan to begin selling meat for the first time in its history. In a community so progressive that it is known as "Berkeley East," this proposal ignited a furious controversy. Sadly, the membership approved it, and the co-op now sells meat. In the debate leading up to the vote, the Dalai Lama's diet was frequently cited as proof that eating meat is both ethically and ecologically acceptable.

As a practicing Tibetan Buddhist, I believe that the Dalai Lama is a great bodhisattva, an emanation of Avalokiteshvara.

Having studied his teachings extensively and spoken with him about animals and veganism, I believe that he is a teacher of vast kindness and compassion who believes that, given the state of his health, he is doing the best he can with his one-day-on, one-day-off regime. I have no doubt that his vegetarian advocacy is sincere, although I understand why it does not always appear so to others.

I was struck recently by an observation of Jeffrey Moussaieff Masson. "I must say, though, that anything a person does to decrease the number of animals killed is good. I used to sneer at the thought that somebody had decided to give up meat once a week. Now I think it's fine. It's a beginning. Most people who begin take the next step."[19] I pray that His Holiness will take the next step by seeking more enlightened medical advice than he has received in the past. And then I pray that he will reconcile his actual diet with the diet that—as he himself recognizes—his religion and his compassion call for. In the meantime, it is important for us as Buddhists to remember that in Buddhism—even in the Vajrayana, which places great emphasis on the guru—the teachings are more important than the person. The Dalai Lama's teaching is unequivocal. "We must promote vegetarianism. It is extremely important."

CHAPTER 14

THE ROSARY OF LIFE

In addition to the Noble Eightfold Path, which we mentioned earlier, there is another set of guidelines for attaining enlightenment called the *perfections*. "Perfection" in this context refers to completeness, the idea being that complete mastery of these attributes will lead to enlightenment. The Mahayana typically speaks of six perfections, and the Theravada 10.[1] In both lists, the first perfection is *dana*, "giving," which includes three types of gift: food, fearlessness, and dharma. "Food" stands for any kind of material aid and constitutes what we more often call "charity." "Fearlessness" refers to safety or freedom from anxiety; it can include saving someone from death or injury. The two categories are not mutually exclusive; a gift of food is frequently also a gift of fearlessness, as in the case of paying the rent for a family about to be made homeless through eviction. The gift of dharma is the gift of showing, by teaching or personal example, the path to enlightenment that will lead to eternal, unalloyed bliss. The gift of dharma is also the ultimate gift of fearlessness.

Activism—speaking and acting against any form of
exploitation that may cause suffering or death for sentient
beings—is part and parcel of the first perfection. Specifically,
it is the gift of fearlessness and may also, as in the case of sanctuaries, include the gift of food. The spirit that infuses dana,
Buddhist generosity, is the spirit of ahimsa that desires to
bring an end to the harm that is done in the world; it is likewise the spirit of the great compassion that desires to bring an
end to all of the world's suffering. Dana is compassion at work
in the world, and activism is dana practiced on as large a scale
as we are able. Activism aspires to reduce suffering by changing at least part of the world.

"Aha!" some readers will exclaim. "That's where your
chain gets wrapped around the axle. Buddhism isn't about
changing the world. Buddhism is about changing yourself."
And they will call to mind the teaching that there are two ways
to protect your feet when you walk. You can cover the whole
world with rubber or you can cover the soles of your feet with
rubber.[2] The problem with this approach by itself is that it is
devoid of compassion. Your rubber-coated feet may be safe,
but other people's feet are being injured every day. What can
you do to help them?

"That's easy!" these readers will reply. "You show them
how to cover their feet, as well." In other words, you give the
gift of dharma. And this is where the metaphor breaks down—
not the original metaphor, but the new, extended edition that
defends quietism and condemns activism. It is quicker, easier,
and cheaper to cover everyone's feet than to cover the surface
of the earth. While you teach people to make shoes, stopgap
measures to protect their feet are neither needed nor available.
But, unlike shoes, enlightenment takes a very long time, many
lifetimes, in fact; and in the meantime, living beings continue
to suffer dreadfully in samsara in myriad ways. Stopgap meas-

ures are absolutely necessary. And that is where the gifts of food and fearlessness enter the picture. That is where activism becomes a vital component of Buddhist practice.

Meditate or Demonstrate?

Mahayana teachings distinguish between "aspiring bodhichitta," which is like planning a trip, and "engaged bodhichitta," which is like actually getting into your car and starting to drive. Aspiring bodhichitta is the essential preparation for engaged bodhichitta, but it is only a preliminary. Engaged bodhichitta is what gets you to your destination. Compassionate feelings are to the great compassion as a block of marble is to the Venus de Milo; they are raw material, nothing more, nothing less. Compassion becomes real when it becomes active in the world.

A more elaborate form of the quietist claim is that activism is a waste of time because it treats only the symptom. The cause of suffering is built into the structure of samsara and the end of suffering is found only in nirvana. Therefore, we Buddhists should spend our time in meditation, not activism, because only when we achieve enlightenment ourselves will we be in a position to help all sentient beings reach nirvana. Those who make this argument act as if the gift of dharma were the entirety of the First Perfection. They ignore the gifts of food and fearlessness, which are also taught as Buddhist virtues. Two of the three forms of Buddhist giving involve the relief of suffering in samsara. For any being who suffers, even transient relief is a blessing; and no one with true compassion should refuse to offer temporary relief when it is needed. We should never take our eyes off the goal of enlightenment for all sentient beings; but we should likewise not use nirvana as a screen to shield ourselves from having to deal with the suffering of beings while they remain subject to the vicissitudes of karma.

There is an old saying that everyone is either part of the problem, part of the solution, or part of the landscape. Obviously, it is contrary to Buddhist teachings on compassion to be part of the problem. But it is also contrary to Buddhist teaching for practitioners to remain part of the landscape while we seek enlightenment. If you fell and broke your leg, how would you feel if others refused to help you because they were too busy seeking enlightenment? Would you find much comfort in their promise to help end all of your suffering once they became enlightened?

Tony Page speaks to precisely this point in his remarkable book *Buddhism and Animals.* "Every person who feels any affinity with the Bodhisattva ideal, particularly, will surely feel the necessity of speaking out on behalf of the oppressed and victimized—whether they be in human or animal form. . . . The vital Buddhist practices of meditation and spiritual study should not be used as a means of cutting ourselves off from empathy with others, but for bringing us closer to them."[3]

The Venerable Mahathera Narada tells us that "Buddhism teaches its followers to elevate the lowly, help the poor, the needy and the forlorn, tend the sick, comfort the bereaved, pity the wicked, and enlighten the ignorant."[4] It was precisely this impulse that led Thich Nhat Hanh to promote "engaged Buddhism," which encourages Buddhist practitioners to work for social justice as well as enlightenment.

Engaged Buddhism

Engaged Buddhism grew out of Thich Nhat Hanh's experiences as a young Zen monk during the American war against Vietnam. It was born in the midst of intense suffering when

Nhat Hanh, Sister Chan Khong, and others who joined them realized that meditation and prayer alone were an incomplete response to the torture, killing, and destruction that were immolating their country. And so, like Gandhi and King, they added the gifts of food and fearlessness to the gift of spiritual teaching and became nonviolent activists.

In the four decades that have followed, engaged Buddhism has become a familiar part of the Buddhist landscape, tending to focus on three issues: world peace, social justice, and protection of the environment. When I make that point to people in conversation, they often get a perplexed look on their faces. "Well, yes, I mean, what else is there?"

What else is there? There are 48 billion land animals slaughtered every year for food, plus an additional 14 billion fish, mollusks, and crustaceans. There are factory farms where chickens spend their entire lives crowded into cages so small they cannot spread their wings and female pigs spend their adulthood either pregnant or nursing and lying on concrete floors in iron cages so cramped they cannot stand up. There are laboratories where rabbits are blinded by caustic chemicals squirted into their eyes without anesthesia or analgesics, and mice are killed by having these same chemicals pumped into their stomachs. For sheer scope and depth of suffering, there is no social injustice that can begin to compare with human oppression of nonhuman animals. There are none who need the gift of fearlessness more desperately than the animals.

Five Principles for Buddhism Engaged on Behalf of Animals
Buddhism values the life and happiness of all living beings equally. There is no hierarchy of moral value. Therefore, Buddhist animal activism strives to protect all sentient beings and the natural world on which we all depend. This implies an end to the use of animals for human pleasure or benefit, the pro-

tection of the environment, the preservation of wilderness, and the sustainable use of natural resources.

Buddhist animal activism is motivated by lovingkindness and compassion, not anger, hatred, or despair. Our goal is not to win, but to win people over. Our compassion extends to the oppressors as well as to the oppressed, but this does not compromise our determination to end all exploitation and abuse of animals.

Buddhist action on behalf of animals is a nonviolent expression of maha-karuna, the great compassion. Our activism must not only state our ethical principles, it must embody them, as well. Our speech is clear and uncompromising; this is our practice of ahimsa toward the victims of oppression. But our speech is also free of rancor; this is our practice of ahimsa toward the oppressors. Our demonstrations are open and welcoming, not threatening or intimidating. Hostility is met with gentleness. Rescues are conducted nonviolently, without gratuitous destruction of property. Campaigns are intended to educate, not intimidate.

In accordance with the principle of skillful means (*upaya*), Buddhist animal activism is carefully thought out to advance the cause of the animals without generating a backlash that overshadows any good that was accomplished. This does not mean being afraid to make people uncomfortable. Animal abuse is so ingrained in our individual and social consciousness that in order to make progress, we must sometimes cause discomfort. But this is the discomfort that is generated by appeals to conscience, never the discomfort that is generated by anger, threats, and insults.

Buddhist animal activism is not about us, and it is not about the abusers. It is about the animals. Their suffering and the end of their suffering is always the primary focus of animal activism as Buddhist practice.

Activism in the Dharma Community

Our relationship to our dharma community calls for a different kind of activism than is needed in the broader society. Here, in the intimacy of our spiritual fellowship, the most effective activism is often the example of our lives. Our teachers and fellow dharma practitioners must see our lives as expressions of the great compassion that the Buddhadharma summons us all to develop. But sometimes seeing will not be enough. Often we will encounter situations where we will need to explain why we do not eat meat, eggs, or dairy. And in doing so, in accordance with the principle of skillful means, we must be clear and unequivocal in speaking out on behalf of the sentient beings who are suffering and dying.

Buddhism is the most gentle of religions, which is one of the reasons I was attracted to it in the first place. But it is possible for an excess of gentleness to be inappropriate to the circumstances. Many vegetarian Buddhists are almost apologetic about their diet. When offered meat, they decline it; but if asked why, they mumble something innocuous and change the subject. In most cases, this excess of modesty arises from the fear that a frank espousal of compassionate vegetarianism would be construed as an implied criticism of meat-eating Buddhists, including teachers who eat meat.

Eating animal products is wrong, even when the person doing it is a teacher—perhaps even more so because our teachers are a living teaching, in obedience to which the rest of us shape our lives. And when we shrink from saying that these things are wrong, we become the lesser for the failure of our compassion, and in us the Buddhist community also becomes lesser. When it is necessary to do so, the blessed Buddhadharma calls us to risk offending some of our fellow practitioners in order to avoid the greater sin of abandoning the sentient beings who are most in need of our voice. The great

scandal of contemporary Buddhism is that so few practitioners are willing to speak out against meat-eating.

The Rosary of Life

Transforming the world implies transforming ourselves. If we
hope to reduce the suffering of sentient beings we must overcome habits and cravings that cause us to add to their suffering. If you have the health, education, motivation, and leisure
to read this book, you have been blessed with a precious
human birth, as I have been. It is up to us to decide: Will we
use what remains of this precious human birth to string a
rosary of death? Or will we use it to string a rosary of life? As
the story of Angulimala tells us, it is never too late to change.

We string a bead on our rosary of life when we adopt a
companion animal from a shelter instead of buying from a
breeder or pet store.

We string a bead on our rosary of life when we spay or
neuter our companion animals to ensure that no additional
dogs or cats come into the world while millions are being
killed every year because there are no homes for them.

We string a bead on our rosary of life when we give up
hunting and fishing and when we post our land so that no one
else can turn it into a killing ground.

We string a bead on our rosary of life when we refuse to
seek our pleasure in the suffering of animals in zoos, theme
parks, circuses, rodeos, horse races, or dog races.

We string a bead on our rosary of life when we drive more
slowly and carefully at dusk and after dark to lessen the
chance of hitting a frightened animal who may dart across the
road in our headlights.

We string a bead on our rosary of life when we learn to
share the space that we call "ours" with others who may
depend on it for their lives. We allow the deer, rabbits, rac-

coons, opossums, and moles to browse in our gardens and dig their tunnels under our lawns, and we do not set out traps or poisons.

We string a bead on our rosary of life when we secure our homes to exclude mice, bats, squirrels and other critters rather than carelessly letting them find a way in and then killing or "relocating" them after they have set up housekeeping. (Some "relocation" services simply kill the animals once they are out of our sight. And many animals cannot survive relocation.)

We string a bead on our rosary of life when we buy household and personal products that contain no animal ingredients and have not been tested on animals.

We string a bead on our rosary of life when speak out against the cruelty and killing that define our relationship with beings in the animal realm: when we write a letter to the editor; when we volunteer our time or contribute money to a group that is working for animal protection; when we call a radio talk show and describe the suffering of animals in laboratories; when we pass out leaflets that depict the suffering of animals in circuses; and when we request that meals and refreshments served at our dharma center not include the bodies of our murdered neighbors. The animals cannot speak on their own behalf; they cannot picket or demonstrate; they cannot vote, and they cannot contribute to political campaigns. They are counting on us to be their voice.

Most of all, we string beads on our rosary of life when we decide that no living being will have to be imprisoned and killed to make our food and clothing. We don't eat meat, eggs, dairy products, or honey. We don't wear fur, leather, wool, or silk. This requires a little retraining—we have to find the stores and Internet sites that sell comfortable and attractive non-leather shoes; we have to develop some new grocery shopping habits—but we don't have to do it all at once. I was a vegetarian for over a year before I became a vegan by ridding my life of eggs, dairy, leather, wool, and silk. What matters is that we take the first steps and continue moving in the right direction. In modern American society, no one can live as a perfect vegan, but we can all do our best, and we can always try to do better today than we did yesterday. Adopting a cruelty-free lifestyle is not painful, not difficult, and does not empty our lives of pleasure. Quite the opposite, it fills our lives with joy. Eating and dressing, which used to be meaning-less acts, are now filled with profound meaning. Every time we sit down to a vegetarian meal, every time we put on a pair of non-leather shoes, we are engaging in a dharma practice that saves the lives of sentient beings and promotes our own spiritual progress. *There is nothing that you and I can do that will ease the suffering of animals more than refusing to eat their bodies or wear their skins.* It is the most important step that we can take to make our practice a blessing to all sentient beings while they remain here in samsara.

NOTES

Introduction
1. Kjolhede, in Tworkov, p. 58.
2. Rahula, 1978, p. 46. Dr. Rahula is quoting the words of the Buddha from the *Mahaparinibbana Sutta* (*Digha Nikaya,* 16).
3. In recent years, some scholars have suggested the more recent dates of c. 480–400 BCE, but most still accept the traditional dating. See Conze, pp. 8–9; Harvey, 1990, p. 9; EEPR, p. 332; and Keown, p. 266.
4. As wealthy aristocrats, they had, of course, no material worries. In later years, the Buddha was reconciled with his family. His step-mother and son abandoned the worldly life and joined the Buddhist sangha.

Chapter 1: The Rosary of Death
1. The story of Angulimala is well known in both Theravada and Mahayana Buddhism. For this retelling, I have relied primarily on *The Angulimala Sutta, Majjhima Nikaya,* 86, in the excellent translation of Ajahn Thanissaro Bhikkhu, a Theravadin monk in the Thai tradition and founder and abbot of the Metta Forest Monastery in California.
2. FARM, 2002. The statistics were compiled from reports issued by the National Agricultural Statistics Service (NASS) of the U.S. Department of Agriculture.
3. Ibid. The statistics were compiled from reports issued by the United Nations Food and Agriculture Organization (FAO).
4. Food and Agriculture Organization.
5. Phelps. The estimate is based on statistics published by the U.S. Fish and Wildlife Service and state wildlife agencies.
6. NAVS. This is a conservative estimate. Since there is no legal requirement to estimate the number of rats and mice used in research and product testing, the actual number is unknown. The North American Anti-Vivisection Society says simply "tens of millions."
7. HSUS. This is a very conservative estimate. Other experts in com-

panion animal issues have told me that the actual number of animals killed in shelters may be twice that. Not included, of course, are the millions of homeless dogs and cats who are killed by cars, predators, disease, and malnutrition.

8. Greyhound Protection League.
9. Goydon and Kindel, p. 2.
10. Ibid., p. 3.
11. Green.
12. Braunstein.
13. Clifton.

Chapter 2: Life on the Farm

1. Patterson, pp. 56–61.
2. Lyman, p. 11.
3. Ibid., pp. 184–185.
4. Scully, p. 251.
5. Masson, p. 138.
6. Lyman, pp. 55–56.
7. Mason and Singer, pp. 77–78.
8. Sometimes one cage serves both purposes. The primary difference between the two is that the back end of a farrowing pen is slightly modified to facilitate birth.
9. Scully, pp. 265, 267. Masson, pp. 38–40.
10. Masson, pp. 17–53; Scully, pp. 247–282.
11. Davis, p. 100.
12. Ibid.
13. Mason and Singer, p. 55.
14. Davis, p. 62.
15. Mason and Singer, p. 24.
16. Davis, pp. 56–65.
17. Ibid., pp. 65–71.
18. Ibid., p. 105.
19. Singer, pp. 129–139.
20. Ibid. , p. 137.
21. Masson, p. 135.
22. Ibid., p. 140.
23. Ibid., p. 145.
24. Eisnitz, p. 82. In January 2004 the U.S. Department of Agriculture, reacting to the appearance of mad cow disease in the United States, issued an order banning the slaughter of downers for human consumption. This is a significant step forward, but it will not eliminate the situation described here. Many cows who are able to walk when they are shipped, cannot when they arrive, and downers may still be shipped for slaughter as food for companion animals and other uses.

25. Ibid., p. 128.
26. Ibid., p. 265.
27. Scully, p. 282.
28. Ibid., p. 283.
29. Davis, pp. 110–111.
30. Ibid., p. 112.
31. Ibid., p. 113.
32. Ibid., p. 116.
33. Davis, p. 115.
34. Ibid.

Chapter 3: Mother Beings

1. Bekoff, 2002, p. 109. Professor Bekoff is quoting from "The Wild into the World: An Interview with Rick Bass," *International Society for Literature and the Environment,* 5:101, 1998.
2. Bekoff, 2002, p. 108.
3. Ibid.
4. "Do Fish Feel Pain," *University of Liverpool News,* April 30, 2003. <http://www.liv.ac.uk/pro/news/trouttrauma.htm>.
5. Buddhists and those who have studied Buddhism will recognize immediately that I am alluding to the doctrine of "no-self" (*anatman, anatta*). This doctrine is central to the Buddhist understanding of how we gain enlightenment, and I am not trying to downplay its importance. But it has little direct bearing on our subject. A bit farther on, I will discuss at length arguments that would justify killing animals on the basis of "emptiness."
6. Lama Kalsang was quoting his own teacher, Deshung Rinpoche.
7. *The Dhammapada,* 129–130.
8. Narada, p. 222. For a description of some of the evidence for reincarnation from a Buddhist perspective, see Sogyal Rinpoche, p. 84ff. The best-known Western collector of evidence for rebirth is Dr. Ian Stevenson of the University of Virginia, author of *Twenty Cases Suggestive of Reincarnation.*
9. Keown, 2003, "Rebirth," p. 235.
10. Rabten, p. 103.
11. I first heard this story from my teacher, Lama Kalsang Gyaltsen. It can be found, with minor variations, in many sources.

Chapter 4: Reason and Rights

1. Harvey, 2000, p. 151.
2. Behaviorists do not so much deny animal sentience as decline, on epistemological grounds, to consider any subjective phenomenon a valid subject for scientific inquiry.
3. Bentham, p. 311. Emphasis in original.

4. Ibid.
5. Lewis, p. 134.
6. Ibid., p. 135.
7. Ibid., p. 136.
8. Ibid.
9. Ibid., p. 137. Lewis adopted this view for theological reasons (He was trying to explain how a God who is all-good and all-powerful could permit animals to suffer when they are not guilty of any sin and cannot be improved spiritually by suffering.), and one gets the impression that in his heart of hearts he didn't really believe it himself. Unfortunately, it has had a great deal of influence, as has his bizarre notion—also adopted for theological reasons—that domestication is the natural state of animals and wildness an aberration. Nevertheless, C. S. Lewis should be given credit for campaigning actively against vivisection.
10. Hendrickx.
11. In fairness to Dr. Hendrickx, the main thrust of her article, which in Italian is entitled "For a More Just Relationship with Animals," is to condemn the cruelty of factory farms and vivisection laboratories that perform experiments that have no real likelihood of improving human health. (She is not prepared to concede that cruelty to animals outweighs potential benefit to humans.) Although it does not go nearly far enough, the article is still a significant step forward for Catholic theology.
12. Singer, in Coetzee et al., p. 87.

Chapter 5: The Great Compassion
1. Rahula, 1978, p. 49.
2. Gunaratana, pp. 65–66.
3. Narada, pp. 182–183.
4. Rahula, 1978, p. 46. *Panna* is Pali. The Sanskrit equivalent is *prajna*.
5. Rahula, 1974, p. 137.
6. Rahula, 1978, p. 46.
7. Dalai Lama, 1996, p. 67.
8. *The Dhammapada*, 129–132.
9. Harvey, 2000, p. 68.
10. Thurman, p. 123. Emphasis in original.
11. Snelling, p. 48.
12. Harvey, 1990, p. 202.
13. Saddhatissa, pp. 59–60.
14. Nhat Hanh, 1987, p. 42.
15. The eight steps are: 1) right view, 2) right aspiration, 3) right speech, 4) right conduct, 5) right livelihood, 6) right effort, 7) right mindfulness, and 8) right meditative concentration.

16. Saddhatissa, pp. 46–47.
17. Nhat Hanh, 1987, p. 40.
18. Lawrence, p. 289. Emphasis added.
19. Zimmer, pp. 105, 495.
20. Ashoka, "Pillar Edict 7."
21. Ashoka, "Rock Edict 2."
22. Ashoka, "Pillar Edict 2."
23. Ashoka, "Rock Edict 1."
24. Ashoka, "Pillar Edict 5." The translator notes that the identification of some of the animals is "conjectural."
25. Ashoka, "Pillar Edict 7."
26. Ashoka, "Rock Edict 1."
27. Chapple, p. 30.

Chapter 6: Thus Have I Heard

1. Zimmer, pp. 491–492; Snelling, 1991, pp. 75–77. The details of the story vary according to the source, but the broad picture is always the same.
2. Snelling, 1991, p. 78; Conze, p. 8.
3. Alternatively, that claim may have been inserted into the Pali Canon to discredit the Mahayana scriptures, which are in Sanskrit.
4. Gethin, pp. 41–42. See also Keown, 2003, "Pali," p. 209.
5. Snelling, 1991, p. 77.
6. Zimmer, pp. 466–467.
7. Conze, pp. 8–9.
8. Another so-called Fourth Buddhist Council, which Theravadins reject, was held in Kashmir or Punjab around 100 CE.
9. Gethin, p. 43.
10. Suzuki, p. 212.
11. Ibid. "Bodhisattva" here means a dedicated follower, a disciple. Parenthetical numbers refer to page numbers in the standard Sanskrit edition, which have come to function much as chapter and verse citations function in Bible study.
12. Ibid. "Mahasattva" means "great being." It is often coupled with "bodhisattva."
13. Ibid. Bracketed text in these quotations was added by Dr. Suzuki for the sake of clarity in English, which is a much less elliptical language than Sanskrit. Otherwise, all bracketed material is by me and followed by my initials (NP).
14. Suzuki, p. 215. Rishis were ancient Indian holy men. The Buddha is saying that from the earliest times, highly realized spiritual seekers have avoided meat.
15. Nhat Hanh, 1998, pp. 62–79. Also Lawrence, pp. 288–289.
16. Suzuki, p. 217. Rakshasas are flesh-eating demons. They are por-

trayed as unhappy beings who spread misfortune and misery to all with whom they come in contact.

17. Ibid.
18. Suzuki, p. 219.
19. Ibid., p. 220. By "terrific," Dr. Suzuki means "terrifying." In Buddhist teaching, the hells are places where negative karma is "matured" or "exhausted," allowing the individual to be reborn in a higher realm and resume her pilgrimage toward Nirvana. It's what we would call "a learning experience."
20. Ibid.
21. Ibid., p. 221.
22. "The Scripture of Brahma's Net," in *Buddhist Writings,* translated by Rev. Hubert Nearman, O.B.C. Shasta Abbey, California, 1994, pp. 127–128. Quoted in Page, p. 131.
23. Goddard, p. 264. "Samadhi" refers to a deep meditative state that only enlightened beings can attain in a pure and stable form. A "Raksha" is the same as a "Rakshasa." "This triple world" refers to samsara.
24. Ibid., p. 265.
25. *The Mahayana Mahaparinirvana Sutra,* translated by Kosho Yamamoto. The Karinbunko, Obe City, Japan, 1973–1975, p. 91. Quoted in Page, pp. 139–140.
26. Ibid. Quoted in Page, pp. 141–142.
27. *Middle Length Discourses,* p. 474. (*Jivaka Sutta, Majjhima Nikaya* 55:5.)
28. Page, p. 123. Emphasis in original.
29. Kapleau, 1981, pp. 29–33.
30. *Middle Length Discourses,* p. 476. (*Jivaka Sutta, Majjhima Nikaya* 55.12.)
31. Nhat Hanh, 1997, p. 68.
32. Ibid., 1992, p. 82.

Chapter 7: The Last Supper

1. The schism had social and political implications that are still only poorly understood, and makes it clear that the Buddha was much more deeply involved in the religious and generational politics of his day than is generally recognized. I have not attempted here to provide a full and rounded description of the schism, but only to discuss its relevance to our topic. As earlier, 500 is a conventional number not to be taken literally. It means "a great many." The schism of Devadatta is described in the Vinaya Pitaka. See Schumann, pp. 232–243; Armstrong, pp. 164–172; Nhat Hanh, 1991, pp. 488–508.
2. Kapleau, 1981, pp. 29–33.
3. *The Mahayana Mahaparinirvana Sutra,* translated by Kosho

Yamamoto. The Karinbunko, Obe City, Japan, 1973–1975, p. 91. Quoted in Page, pp. 139–140. Italics added.

4. *Long Discourses*, pp. 256 ff. and note 417. (*Mahaparinibbana Sutta, Digha Nikaya* 16.4.17 ff.).
5. *Long Discourses*, p. 256, note 417. Kapleau, 1981, pp. 24–25. Page, pp. 119–122.
6. Keown, 2003, "sukara-maddava," pp. 281–282. Kapleau, 1981, pp. 24–25; Page, pp. 119–122; Schumann, p. 247. Armstrong, p. 179.
7. *Long Discourses*, pp. 571–572, notes 417, 418.
8. Keown, 2003, "sukara-maddava," p. 281.
9. Kapleau, 1981, pp. 24–25.
10. Ibid., p. 24.
11. Nhat Hanh, 1991, p. 553.
12. She cites Michael Edwardes, a highly regarded Indologist.
13. Armstrong, p. 179.

Chapter 8: The Branch of Sorrow

1. Page, p. 143. Italics in original.
2. Ibid.
3. Ibid., pp. 143–144. Italics in original.
4. Jones, p. 123.
5. For an analysis of the roles of government and hunting vis-à-vis wildlife management and wildlife populations, see Phelps.
6. Jones, p. 124.
7. Ibid.
8. Ibid.
9. Ibid.
10. *The Dhammapada*, 131.
11. Geshe Kelsang Gyatso, p. 145. See also Geshe Rabten and Geshe Dargyay, p. 86.
12. Website of the Primate Freedom Project. <www.primatefreedom.com/centers/wisconupdate1.html>
13. Page, pp. 153–154.
14. Ashvaghosha, *Buddha-karita* (*The Deeds of the Buddha*), quoted in Page, p. 156.
15. Saddhatissa, p. 60.

Chapter 9: Precious Human Birth

1. There are other systems that divide samsara into varying numbers of realms. But they all describe the same territory and differ primarily according to the purpose of the analysis and into how much detail the realms are subdivided. One approach, for example, describes three sets of realms in samsara, the desire realms, the form realms,

and the formless realms. The desire realms include the hell realms, the realm of the hungry ghosts, the animal realm, the human realm, the realm of the demi-gods, and several subdivisions of the god realm. The remainder of the god realm is divided between the form realms and the formless realms.

2. Beings in the formless realms have no bodies, only minds.
3. I.e., wisdom, which, being a function of Buddha Nature rather than the human mind, is available to all sentient beings, if only they knew how to access it and were motivated to do so.
4. Kalu Rinpoche, p. 91. "Other states of existence" refers to the four invisible realms. By "opportunities and freedoms," Rinpoche means what I was taught by my teacher to call "freedoms and endowments." Tibetan Buddhism has not yet developed a fully standardized English vocabulary.
5. Ibid., p. 25.
6. Ray, p. 267.
7. Sometimes spelled Dezhung Rinpoche.
8. Deshung Rinpoche, p. 103.
9. Tellingly, I have never in twenty years heard this defense of animal abuse made by an Asian Buddhist or by a Western Buddhist who had studied extensively with an Asian teacher.
10. Dalai Lama, 2002, p. 89.
11. Jamgon Kongtrul Lodro Thaye, p. 3. Italics in original.
12. For an extensive description of animal liberation as it is performed in Tibetan Buddhism, see Zopa Rinpoche, pp. 169–203.
13. Animal Liberation Report, p. 4.

Chapter 10: The Cabbage and the Cow
1. Quoted in Kain, p. 65.
2. Nhat Hanh, 1998, p. 86. With slight variations in wording, he says essentially the same thing whenever he discusses the First Precept. See, for example, Nhat Hanh, 1993, p. 56.
3. Nhat Hanh, 1998, p. 86.
4. Nhat Hanh, 1997, pp. 34–35.
5. Ibid., p. 65.
6. Knowles.
7. Harvey, 1990, p. 99.
8. Nhat Hanh, 1998, pp. 113–114.
9. Ibid., 1993, p. 69.
10. II Corinthians 3:6.

Chapter 11: More Mind Games
1. Chan Khong, in Nhat Hanh et al., p. 157.
2. This analysis was first suggested to me by Paul Shapiro of Compas-

sion Over Killing (COK), a Washington, D.C.–based animal rights organization.

3. Glass, in Tworkov, p. 57.
4. Ibid.
5. Klaper, p. 1. Dr. Klaper believes that inability to metabolize a vegan diet occurs "occasionally," and he is currently conducting a large-scale, longitudinal study to determine how often and from what causes. For more information, visit his website, which is listed under "Websites/Resources," and click on "More Study Details."
6. American Dietetic Association, p. 748.
7. Quoted in Jones, p. 125.
8. *The Dhammapada*, 1.
9. Nhat Hanh, 1997, pp. 34–35.
10. *The Mahayana Mahaparinirvana Sutra,* quoted in Page, p. 140.
11. The Dalai Lama, 2001, p. 14.
12. Lawrence, p. 293.
13. Saddhatissa, p. 60
14. Nhat Hanh, 1993, p. 65.
15. Marcus, p. 164.
16. Ibid.
17. Nhat Hanh, 1993, p. 65.

Chapter 12: The Western Seduction

1. Goldstein, p. 59.
2. *The Brahmajala Sutra,* quoted in Page, p. 131.
3. Goldstein, p. 59.
4. Surya Das, p. 1.
5. Ibid., p. 2.
6. Ibid., p. 3.
7. The meaning of the Fourth Precept, prohibiting "sexual misconduct," is a bit fuzzy. Some teachers, especially in the Tibetan tradition, apply it quite broadly, to preclude, for example, sexual activity in a holy place (a shrine room, temple, etc.), sex during a woman's menstrual period, and any form of sexual relations other than genital-to-genital intercourse between a man and a woman. But most teachers, even in Tibetan Buddhism, would limit sexual misconduct to incest, zoophilia, sexual relations that break a vow, such as a marriage vow or a vow of celibacy, and sexual activity that is coercive or exploitative, including rape and sexual relations with children or people who are mentally deficient. Surya Das certainly had in mind sexual relations between consenting adults who are breaking no vows. Therefore, his answer regarding sex reflects traditional, mainstream Buddhist teaching—which his answers on meat and alcohol do not. (On alcohol, see Nhat Hanh, 1998, pp. 63–65, 75–77.)

8. Nhat Hanh, 1992, p. 82.
9. Surya Das, p. 3.
10. Alcohol and drugs also cause great suffering, which is why they are forbidden by the Precepts, but they are less egregious offenders than killing, which is why the First Precept is preeminent.
11. What follows, of course, is a generalization based on anecdotal evidence. It is by no means universally valid. Soka Gakkai International, for example, is a significant exception.
12. Glass, in Tworkov, p. 57.
13. Ibid. Italics in original.
14. Smith, p. 91.
15. Cleland, p. 25.
16. Ibid.

Chapter 13: The Diamond Vehicle and the Dalai Lama

1. There are no reliable statistics, but there is general agreement that among these three Jainism has the highest proportion of vegetarians.
2. Janet Gyatso, p. 137.
3. Dr. Gyatso is referring to the animal liberation practices that we described earlier.
4. Janet Gyatso, p. 137. The Palas were a family of the Tibetan nobility who were noted patrons of the dharma.
5. Shabkar, p. 232. Jowo Rinpoche is a famous statue of the Buddha in Lhasa. Since Buddhists are instructed to show an image of the Buddha the same respect that they would show the living Buddha, Shabkar is emphasizing that this was an extremely serious vow.
6. Ibid., pp. 327–328.
7. Ibid., p. 349.
8. Patrul Rinpoche, p. 207.
9. Conze, pp. 75, 104–105. See Harvey, 1990, pp. 133–138.
10. Quoted in Khetsun Sangpo Rinpoche, p. 99.
11. Also known as Birwapa, he is even more famous for making the sun stand still in order to avoid paying his bar tab, which he had promised to settle at sunset. A wealthy patron eventually paid Virupa's bill so the sun would go down and he could get some sleep. Stiffing a bartender may not be the most spiritual of deeds, but it has certain advantages over making the sun stand still so you can continue to slaughter people in battle.
12. Lama Kalsang Gyaltsen, in conversation.
13. See Landaw and Weber, pp. 58–59.
14. Unfortunately, this vegetarian practice seems to be honored as much in the breach as in the observance, especially in monasteries that begin every day with a Tara practice. For an extended discussion of Tara, see Landaw and Weber, pp. 79–91.

15. It is also told in his autobiography, *Freedom in Exile,* pp. 179, 184–185. At the time he wrote this, he had not yet adopted his alternating days approach.
16. He had bought live fish from a market and released them in the pond as part of an animal liberation practice of the kind I described earlier.
17. Dalai Lama and Fabien Ouaki, p. 30.
18. Dalai Lama, 2001, *Live in a Better Way,* p. 68.
19. Masson, p. 228.

Chapter 14: The Rosary of Life
1. Both sets are listed in the Glossary under *perfections.* The two lists are simply different ways of dividing up the same spectrum. Likewise, the perfections do not conflict with the Noble Eightfold Path; they are an alternate way of describing the same transformative process.
2. The original teaching says "leather." But this is a vegan book.
3. Page, p. 175.
4. Narada, p. 183.

GLOSSARY OF ANIMAL-RELATED TERMS

Agribusiness: One of the large, often multinational corporations, like Archer Daniels Midland, ConAgra, and Tyson, that now dominate food production throughout the world. Most of the family farms that still survive exist only as subcontractors to large agribusinesses, which set production standards and control prices.

Animal rights: The belief that all animals are entitled to life, liberty and the integrity of their bodies, and that they should be allowed to live according to the dictates of their nature, as free from human interference as possible. Animal rights precludes the exploitation of animals for human pleasure or benefit.

Animal welfare: The belief that animals may be used or killed for human pleasure or benefit, but that they should be subjected to the minimum amount of suffering that is consistent with the purpose for which they are being used. Most animal welfare advocates would ban some forms of extreme animal cruelty, such dog fighting or cock fighting.

Battery cage: A wire cage, rows of which are stacked vertically and horizontally in confinement sheds, in which all laying hens and many broiler chickens spend their entire adult lives. A typical battery cage would confine 4 or 5 chickens in a 12″ by 18″ space, giving the birds no room to turn around or spread their wings.

Broiler chicken: Any chicken raised for meat, rather than to lay eggs. Broiler chickens have been bred to produce an abnormal amount of muscle in a short period of time, and, in effect, constitute a separate breed of chicken.

Cannibalism: The tendency of animals, especially chickens and pigs, to attack one another under the stress of intensive confinement. Debeaking of chickens and tail docking of pigs are common methods of dealing with cannibalism, which does not occur in free-ranging animals.

Chute: A narrow, fenced walkway along which animals enter a slaughterhouse.

Confinement shed: A building in which farmed animals, especially chickens, pigs, and dairy cows, are confined to permit the manipulation of their environment in ways that reduce the unit cost of maintaining them and maximize their production.

Debeaking: Cutting or burning off a chicken's beak, without anesthesia, to keep her from pecking and injuring the other chickens crowded into the battery cage or confinement shed. Pecking leading to injury is a sign of severe emotional distress caused by confinement. There is no need to debeak free-ranging chickens who can move about and organize themselves into a flock.

Downer: An animal who arrives at a slaughterhouse too severely injured, too sick, or too weak to walk up the chute. Downers may be dragged into the slaughterhouse by means of a meat hook embedded in their flesh.

Factory farm: An agricultural facility in which animals are raised in unnatural conditions of intensive confinement using environmental manipulation, drugs, hormone supplements, and mutilation (see *debeaking* and *tail docking*) to generate the maximum profit in the shortest time. First created in the years surrounding World War II, factory farms now dominate world meat, egg, and dairy production.

Farrowing pen: A railed enclosure with a concrete floor in which female breeding pigs on factory farms give birth and nurse their babies. The pen holds the pig immobile, unable to stand or turn over.

Feedlot: A large outdoor pen that holds several hundred to several thousand cattle in intensive confinement so that they can be fed a special diet (including bovine growth hormones, BGH) that will fatten them more quickly than would grazing on a range.

Free-range: An animal not kept in intensive confinement but allowed a minimal amount of freedom in a somewhat natural environment, such as a yard or a pasture.

Gestation crate: A narrow metal cage with a concrete floor in which a female pig is artificially inseminated and in which she stays, immobile, until it is time for her babies to be born, when she may be moved to a *farrowing pen*.

Intensive confinement animal production (*ICAP*): The food industry's term for factory farming.

Laying hen: A hen raised for her eggs rather than her meat.

Speciesism: A word coined by British philosopher Richard Ryder on the model of "racism" and "sexism." It denotes a prejudice against nonhuman animals that is used to justify their exploitation and abuse by humankind.

Spent: An industry term for: 1) laying hens and dairy cows who are too old or too weak to maintain production levels; and 2) female breeding animals who are too old or too weak to become pregnant and carry their babies to term.

Tail docking: Cutting off a pig's tail to keep it from being bitten by other pigs in the confinement shed. Tail biting is a sign of severe emotional distress caused by confinement. There is no need to dock the tails of free-range pigs who can move about and interact normally with other pigs.

Veal calf: A male calf taken from his mother a day or two after birth, placed in a veal crate, and fed a diet lacking in iron to produce the white, tender meat favored by people who eat veal. Veal calves are slaughtered at 14 or 15 weeks old, while they are still babies.

Veal crate: A cage so narrow that the veal calf confined in it cannot lie down or turn around. Veal calves are forced to live their entire lives in these crates to keep them from developing the muscle tone that might make their flesh tough. They are never taken out for exercise.

Vegetarian: Someone who eats no meat. Food that contains no meat. Vegetarians may consume dairy products and sometimes eggs. People who eat chicken or fish are not vegetarians.

Vegan: (VEE-gun) Someone who does not eat, wear, or use animal products, including milk, eggs, honey, silk, and wool; something that does not include animal products.

GLOSSARY OF BUDDHIST TERMS

Ahimsa: (ah-HIM-sah) Nonviolence. The Hindu, Jain, and Buddhist teaching that striving to cause no harm to sentient beings is the foundation of ethical behavior and spiritual growth. (Sanskrit, *a*, "no" and *himsa*, "harm"; Pali, *avihimsa*)

Arhat: (AR-hot; Pali, *arhant*, AR-hahnt; sometimes spelled *arahat* and *arahant*) In Theravada Buddhism, someone who has achieved the great compassion and the great wisdom and attained liberation from samsara. Upon death, arhats enter nirvana and are not reborn in samsara.

Bodhichitta: (BOH-dee-CHEE-tah) A Sanskrit word meaning "enlightened mind" or "enlightened attitude." Strictly speaking, bodhichitta has two components: direct insight into the true nature of reality ("ultimate bodhichitta"); and unalloyed compassion for all sentient beings ("relative bodhichitta"). Often, however, "bodhichitta" is used as shorthand for "relative bodhichitta."

Bodhisattva: (BOH-dee-SAHT-vah; Pali, *Bodhisatta*) A Sanskrit word that literally means "enlightened being." Depending on the context, *bodhisattva* can refer to: 1) a serious Buddhist practitioner; 2) someone who has made significant progress toward developing bodhichitta; 3) someone who has vowed to become a Buddha and is on the path to doing so; or 4) someone who has achieved enlightenment but chooses to remain in samsara to relieve the suffering of sentient beings. Definition 3 is *bodhisattva's* most common meaning in the Theravada, and definition 4 is the most common meaning in the Mahayana.

Buddha: A Sanskrit and Pali title meaning "the enlightened one." The historical Buddha was a north Indian aristocrat named Siddhartha Gautama (sid-HART-uh GO-tuh-muh; Pali, Siddhartha Gotama) (*c.* 566–486 BCE). At the age of 29, he abandoned the worldly life to seek enlightenment, which he attained after six years of practicing meditation and other spiritual disciplines. The remaining 45 years of his life were spent teaching the spiritual path that he had discovered.

Buddhadharma: Buddhist teachings. The spiritual path taught by the Buddha.

Compassion: (Sanskrit-Pali, *karuna*) The desire to relieve the suffering of sentient beings. In Buddhist teachings, it is often coupled with *lovingkindness* (Sanskrit, *maitri*; Pali, *metta*), which is the desire to make other beings happy. In a kind of shorthand, "compassion" is often used to mean both compassion properly so called and lovingkindness.

Dakini: In Tibetan Buddhism, a highly realized female spiritual being who assists Vajrayana practitioners.

Dharma: A Sanskrit word with many meanings. In our context, it identifies the spiritual path taught by the Buddha. The Pali equivalent is *dhamma*.

Dharma practice: Any activity intended to implement Buddhist teachings, ranging from meditation, prayer, and chanting to exercising patience and treating others with kindness.

Enlightenment: The goal of Buddhist practice. Direct, intuitive knowledge of the true nature of reality, which is beyond the ability of our minds to conceptualize or our language to express. Achieving enlightenment allows us to understand that the everyday world as we normally perceive it is illusory. Compassion for all living beings is a prerequisite to enlightenment, while the result of enlightenment is Nirvana.

Hinayana: (HIN-ah-YAH-nah) Buddhist teachings that emphasize personal liberation through strict moral discipline. It is not clear whether there was ever a distinct school of Buddhism called "Hinayana," but, despite a popular misconception, "Hinayana" does not refer to Theravada Buddhism.

Lovingkindness: (Sanskrit, *maitri*; Pali, *metta*) the desire to make other beings happy. It is often linked with compassion, and in a kind of shorthand, "compassion" is sometimes used to mean both compassion narrowly defined and lovingkindness.

Mahayana: (MAH-hah-YAH-nah) the "Northern School" of Buddhism, found in China, Japan, Central Asia, and Vietnam, and including Tibetan Buddhism and Zen.

Mahayana Sutras: A collection of Mahayana Buddhist scriptures originally written in Sanskrit.

Mara: The tempter. The personification of the evil thoughts that exist in all our minds.

Nirvana: The Sanskrit name (the Pali equivalent is *nibbana*) for the perfect, eternal bliss that awaits those who achieve enlightenment.

Pali: (poly) An ancient Indian language derived from Sanskrit.

Pali Canon: Buddhist scriptures written in the Pali language. The Pali Canon is the only collection of scriptures recognized in Theravada Buddhism. Mahayana Buddhism does not reject the Pali Canon but places greater reliance on the Mahayana Sutras.

Perfection: (Sanskrit, *paramita*; Pali, *parami*). A quality or practice essential to attaining enlightenment. The Mahayana usually teaches six perfections and the Theravada 10. The six are: giving, morality, patience, perseverance, meditation, and wisdom. The 10 are giving, morality, renunciation, wisdom, perseverance, patience, sincerity, determination, lovingkindness, and equanimity.

Precepts: The five Buddhist precepts, which form the basis of Buddhist ethics, are: do not kill; do not steal; do not lie; do not commit sexual misconduct; do not use substances that dull or distort the mind.

Refuge Vows: The formal initiation ceremony in all schools of Buddhism. By promising to take refuge in the Buddha, the Dharma, and the Sangha, the initiate becomes a Buddhist.

Samsara: (sahm-SAHR-ah) The everyday world of suffering in which we all must live in a continuous cycle of life, death, and rebirth until we achieve enlightenment.

Sanskrit: The classical literary and religious language of ancient India. Sanskrit is to India as Hebrew, Greek, and Latin are to Europe.

Sangha: (SAHN-gah) A Sanskrit and Pali word with several meanings. Usually, it refers to the community of ordained Buddhist monks and nuns, sometimes known as the "robed sangha." Less often, it may refer to a Buddhist congregation, to the entire community of Buddhist practitioners, or to the buddhas, bodhisattvas, and arhats who have attained enlightenment. The latter is properly called the *Arya Sangha,* "the noble sangha."

Shakyamuni: "The sage of the Shakya clan." A term used to distinguish the historical Buddha, Siddhartha Gautama, from legendary Buddhas of the distant past and anticipated Buddhas of the future.

Shravaka: "Hearer, listener." Although it later acquired additional meanings, when used by the Buddha, *shravaka* means simply "disciple," or "Buddhist."

Skillful Means: (*upaya*) Superior insight into the needs of living beings and the effects of your own actions, so that your lovingkindness and compassion can be effectively put to work helping living beings. Skillful means are developed by studying the dharma, contemplating what you have studied, practicing meditation, and maintaining mindfulness. The ultimate goal of skillful means is to bring all living beings to enlightenment.

Sutra: Sanskrit, a Buddhist scripture containing teachings of the Buddha. The Pali equivalent is *sutta.*

Theravada: (TAIR-ah-VAH-dah) The "Southern School" of Buddhism, found in Sri Lanka and much of southeast Asia.

Tripitaka: (Sanskrit, Pali, "the three baskets") The three principal divisions of Buddhist Scripture, both Theravada and Mahayana. The *Vinaya Pitaka* deals with monastic discipline; the *Sutra Pitaka* (Pali, *Sutta Pitaka*) contains discourses of the Buddha; and the *Abhidharma Pitaka* (Pali, *Abhidhamma Pitaka*) consists of treatises on psychology and metaphysics.

Triple Gem: The Buddha, Dharma, and Sangha. The object of refuge vows.

Vajrayana: (VAJ-rah-YAH-nah) Also known as "Mantrayana," or "Secret Mantra Teachings." Esoteric teachings of Tibetan Buddhism, characterized by the use of meditation techniques built around guided visualizations.

Wisdom: (Sanskrit, *prajna*; Pali, *panna*) Direct, intuitive insight into the true nature of reality. The attainment of this insight through meditation and other spiritual techniques constitutes enlightenment and leads to nirvana. The development of universal compassion is the prerequisite to attaining wisdom.

Yidam: (YIH-dahm) A Tibetan word usually translated "meditational deity." A yidam is a transcendent being who is typically conceived as the personification of a particular virtuous quality, such as compassion (Avalokiteshvara), wisdom (Manjushri), spiritual power (Vajrapani), compassionate activity in samsara (Tara), etc. Vajrayana meditation practice includes guided visualizations of one or more yidams as a way of developing spiritual qualities or removing some obstacle, such as ill health, to progress on the spiritual path. Yidams are more akin to patron saints than to gods and goddesses.

Zen: The Japanese name for a form of Mahayana Buddhism that originated in China (where it is known as *Chan*). Also found in Korea and Vietnam, Zen emphasizes "sudden enlightenment" in a flash of inspiration that reveals the true nature of reality.

SUGGESTIONS FOR FURTHER READING

Note:
The section on "Buddhism" is intended for non-Buddhist animal activists who are looking for introductions to a subject with which they may be familiar only in the broadest terms. The remaining sections are intended for Buddhists who wish to learn more about animal rights and a vegan lifestyle.

Animal Agriculture

Davis, Karen, *Prisoned Chickens, Poisoned Eggs: An Inside Look at the Modern Poultry Industry.* A readable, authoritative look at the cruelty, environmental destructiveness, and public health dangers in modern industrial chicken farming and egg production.

——. *More Than a Meal: The Turkey in History, Myth, Ritual, and Reality.* The definitive study of the many roles played by the turkey in human society.

Eisnitz, Gail A., *Slaughterhouse.* This book grew out of an undercover investigation of the meat processing industry. It is essential reading for anyone who eats meat or wears leather—as well as anyone who cares about animals.

Lyman, Howard F., *Mad Cowboy: Plain Truth from the Cattle Rancher Who Won't Eat Meat.* The inside story of the modern beef industry.

Mason, Jim, and Peter Singer, *Animal Factories.* Updated Edition. The indispensable guide to the cruelty entailed in modern meat production. (As of January 2004, a third, further updated edition has been promised in the near future.)

Animal Consciousness, Emotions, and Intelligence

Barber, Theodore Xenophon, *The Human Nature of Birds: A Scientific Discovery with Startling Implications.* A well-written, well-documented look at the intelligence and emotions of animals.

Bekoff, Marc, Editor, *The Smile of a Dolphin: Remarkable Accounts of Animal Emotions.* Brief but thought-provoking stories by scientists and researchers document the fresh look that many scientists are taking at animal consciousness and character.

———. *Strolling with Our Kin: Speaking for and Respecting Voiceless Animals.* A book for young people that adults can enjoy and learn from as well. Highly recommended for all ages.

———. *Minding Animals: Awareness, Emotions, and Heart.* If you only read one book on nonhuman intelligence, emotions, and consciousness, this should be it.

Kreisler, Kristin von, *The Compassion of Animals: True Stories of Animal Courage and Kindness.* Accounts of animals displaying love, devotion, compassion, self-sacrifice, and other "higher" emotions collected from around the world by a staff writer for *Reader's Digest.*

———. *Beauty in the Beasts: True Stories of Animals Who Choose to Do Good.* A worthy sequel to *The Compassion of Animals.*

Linden, Eugene, *The Parrot's Lament: And Other True Tales of Animal Intrigue, Intelligence, and Ingenuity.* An accessible, fascinating look at animal intelligence by a well-known science writer.

———. *The Octopus and the Orangutan: New Tales of Animal Intrigue, Intelligence, and Ingenuity.* One of the best of the wave of new books that are breaking down the myth of human uniqueness and animal stupidity.

Masson, Jeffrey Moussaieff and Susan McCarthy, *When Elephants Weep: The Emotional Lives of Animals.* The book that made it respectable to talk about animals having emotions.

Masson, Jeffrey Mousiaeiff, *The Pig Who Sang to the Moon: The Emotional World of Farm Animals.* An engaging, persuasive look at the complex emotional lives of the sensitive, intelligent animals whom we imprison and slaughter for food.

Tobias, Michael, and Kate Solisti-Mattelon, Editors, *Kinship with the Animals.* An outstanding collection of thoughtful and thought-provoking essays by thinkers and activists who are on the cutting edge of redefining the human-nonhuman relationship.

Animal Rights

Cavalieri, Paola, *The Animal Question: Why Nonhuman Animals Deserve Human Rights.* An intellectually rigorous defense of animal rights.

DeGrazia, David, *Animal Rights: A Very Short Introduction.* Part of Oxford University Press's *Very Short Introductions* series, this is the best brief overview and analysis of animal rights theory that I have encountered. By an Associate Professor of Philosophy at George Washington University.

Donovan, Josephine, and Carol J. Adams, *Beyond Animal Rights: A Feminist Caring Ethic for the Treatment of Animals.* Essays on compassion as the proper basis for our relationship with nonhuman animals.

Dunayer, Joan, *Animal Equality: Language and Liberation.* An eye-opening analysis of the speciesism in our language and the ways that it affects our thinking about animals.

Fox, Michael, *Inhumane Society: The American Way of Exploiting Animals.*

Although in my view it does not go far enough (Dr. Fox seems to believe, for example, that there is such a thing as "humane slaughter."), this is still one of the best books available on the status and treatment of animals in America. By a veterinarian and vice president of the Humane Society of the United States.

Francione, Gary, *Introduction to Animal Rights: Your Child or the Dog?* An accessible, comprehensive introduction to the theory and practice of animal rights. By an attorney who is a leading proponent of legal rights for animals. The Appendix, "Twenty Questions (And Answers)," alone is worth the purchase price.

Marcus, Erik, *Vegan: The New Ethics of Eating.* A clear and well-documented argument for a vegan diet as the cure for the cruelty of factory farming and the plague of world hunger, and a convincing description of its benefits for human health and the environment.

Patterson, Charles, *Eternal Treblinka: Our Treatment of Animals and the Holocaust.* How systematized violence against animals prepares us for systematized violence against human beings. A groundbreaking study by a highly respected Holocaust scholar.

Regan, Tom, *The Case for Animal Rights.* The classic work by the leading philosopher of animal rights. Essential reading for anyone interested in academic philosophy and animal rights.

———.*Empty Cages: Facing the Challenge of Animal Rights.* An excellent, non-technical introduction to animal rights. Especially recommended for people who see the fundamental justice of the animal rights position but are reluctant for any of a variety of reasons to identify with it.

Singer, Peter, *Animal Liberation.* Second Edition. The book that on its initial publication in 1975 jump-started the modern animal rights movement. Still the indispensable classic.

Stallwood, Kim W., Editor, *A Primer on Animal Rights: Leading Experts Write about Animal Cruelty and Exploitation.* An anthology of articles from the regrettably defunct *Animals' Agenda* magazine, which was the leading journal of the animal protection movement for two decades. Covers everything from companion animals to hunting to factory farming.

Animals and Spirituality

Carman, Judy, *Peace to All Beings: Veggie Soup for the Chicken's Soul.* A profound and inspiring meditation on our relationship with animals, drawing on a wide range of spiritual traditions and holding out hope for the evolution of humanity from *homo sapiens* to *homo ahimsa*.

Kowalski, Gary, *The Souls of Animals.* A brilliant and moving look at the personhood of nonhuman animals by a Unitarian-Universalist minister who concludes that "Animals, like us, are living souls. They are not things. With us they share in the gifts of consciousness and life. In a wonderful and inexpressible way, therefore, God is present in all creatures." Making allowances for the vocabulary, this book is open, ecumenical, and as relevant to Buddhists as to Christians.

Randour, Mary Lou, *Animal Grace: Entering a Spiritual Relationship with Our Fellow Creatures.* An elegant, intelligent, and ecumenical reflection on animals, nonviolence, and the life of the spirit.

Buddhism

Carrithers, Michael, *Buddhism: A Very Short Introduction.* Part of Oxford's *Very Short Introductions Series.* An excellent introduction that focuses primarily on the Pali Canon and Theravada Buddhism.

Erricker, Clive, *Buddhism,* New Edition. Part of the popular *Teach Yourself* series. A broadly based, comprehensive description that quotes extensively from Buddhist sources.

Harvey, Peter, *An Introduction to Buddhism: Teachings, History, and Practices.* A thorough, in-depth review that is still accessible to the general reader by a leading contemporary Buddhist scholar. Highly recommended for those with a serious interest in Buddhism.

Smith, Huston, and Philip Novak, *Buddhism: A Concise Introduction.* This is an expansion of the "Buddhism" section of Huston Smith's classic *The World's Religions.* Overall, it is a remarkably intelligent, insightful and sensitive introduction to Buddhism—with the exception of Tibetan Buddhism, which it treats as a cultural curiosity rather than a vital spiritual tradition, seriously distorting the teachings in the process.

Snelling, John, *Way of Buddhism.* Part of the *Thorsons Way of* series. A balanced approach that covers both teachings and history in a clear, readable format.

Thaye, Lama Jampa, *Way of Tibetan Buddhism.* An outstanding introduction. Easily understandable by those unfamiliar with Buddhism.

Buddhism and Animal Rights

Amey, Rosemary A., "Animal Rights and the Dhammapada." An insightful and well-written analysis of an extremely popular Buddhist scripture (from the Pali Canon) that is recognized by all traditions. Amey makes a persuasive case from the *Dhammapada* that animal rights is woven into the fabric of Buddhism. Available at www.rosemaryamey.com/dhamma.

Berry, Rynn, *Food for the Gods: Vegetarianism and the World's Religions.* An outstanding survey of the teachings of nine world religions, including Buddhism, on animals and vegetarianism. Berry couples an insightful essay on each religion with an interview with a representative of that religion.

Hiatt, Sky, "Buddhism and Vegetarianism." In *VegNews: Your Monthy Vegetarian Newspaper,* December 2002. Focusing mostly on Tibetan Buddhism, this is an incisive look at the Buddhist rationales for meat-eating.

Kapleau, Philip, *To Cherish All Life: A Buddhist Guide for Becoming Vegetarian.* The classic work on Buddhism and animal rights by the prominent American Zen Master and author of *The Three Pillars of Zen.*

Lawrence, Kate, "Nourishing Ourselves, Nourishing Others: How Mindful Food Choices Reduce Suffering." In *Mindfulness in the Marketplace: Consuming with Compassion,* edited by Alan Hunt Badner. An elegant argument for Buddhist vegetarianism by a student of Thich Nhat Hanh. Also available at the website of the Society of Ethical and Religious Vegetarians, <www.serv-online.org>.

McGuire, Tom, "Killing Them Softly: The Buddhist Rationale for Eating Animals." In *Satya: A Magazine of Vegetarianism, Environmentalism, Animal Advocacy, and Social Justice,* April 1998. I think McGuire is off target when he says that the Buddha condoned meat-eating, but his assessment of the current situation in the Buddhist community is accurate, unsparing, and still current, while his demolition of the Buddhist arguments used to justify carnivorous eating is right on point. Available at www.satyamag.com/apr98/rationale.html.

Page, Tony, *Buddhism and Animals: A Buddhist Vision of Humanity's Rightful Relationship with the Animal Kingdom.* An exhaustive and authoritative analysis of the Buddhist Scriptures' (both the Pali Canon and the Mahayana Sutras) teachings on animals and all forms of animal exploitation.

Rosen, Steven, *Diet for Transcendence: Vegetarianism and the World's Religions.* An excellent brief introduction to the teachings of eight world religions, including Buddhism, on animals and vegetarianism.

Waldau, Paul, *The Specter of Speciesism: Buddhist and Christian Views of Animals.* A comprehensive and insightful scholarly study of the inroads that speciesism has made into Buddhism and Christianity.

Weintraub, Eileen, "Life as a Vegetarian Tibetan Buddhist Practitioner: A Personal View." Originally published in *Satya: A Magazine of Vegetarianism, Environmentalism, Animal Advocacy, and Social Justice.* A sensitive and knowledgeable review of vegetarianism (and the lack of it) in Tibetan Buddhism by an "insider" who studied in Tibet. Also available at the website of the Society of Ethical and Religious Vegetarians, <www.serv-online.org>.

Companion Animals

Brestrup, Craig, *Disposable Animals: Ending the Tragedy of Throwaway Pets.* A penetrating analysis of our system of treating animals as property.

Hunting

Amory, Cleveland, *Mankind? Our Incredible War on Wildlife.* The statistics are out of date, but you shouldn't read *Mankind?* for the statistics.

After three decades, Cleveland Amory's classic expose of the cruelty and destructiveness of hunting is as on target as when it was first published.

Baker, Ron, *The American Hunting Myth*. An eye-opening description of "wildlife management" in the U.S., together with insightful deconstructions of the arguments most often used to defend hunting.

Phelps, Norm, "A Dying Sport: The State of Hunting in America." Thirty-five-page booklet available from The Fund for Animals that surveys the history, current status, and future of sport hunting.

Vegetarian/Vegan Lifestyle

Note: Food is the ultimate matter of personal taste, and there are so many outstanding vegetarian and vegan cookbooks available that I have not tried to pick and choose among them. A few minutes perusing the Vegetarian Cooking section of your favorite bookstore will tell you far more than I could.

Adams, Carol J., *Living Among Meat Eaters: The Vegetarian's Survival Handbook*. Gentle, insightful, and realistic advice for reducing the stress of becoming vegetarian when you are surrounded by carnivores at home, work, and play.

————. *The Inner Art of Vegetarianism: Spiritual Practices for Body and Soul*. Vegetarianism as a spiritual practice and spiritual practices for vegetarians. Highly recommended for Buddhists, who will find *The Inner Art* healing, inspiring, and entirely compatible with their main practice. Two outstanding companion volumes are also available: *The Inner Art of Vegetarianism Workbook* and *Meditations on the Inner Art of Vegetarianism*.

Marcus, Erik, *Vegan: The New Ethics of Eating*. An excellent introduction to the ethical, ecological, social, and health reasons for adopting a vegan diet.

Moran, Victoria, *Compassion, the Ultimate Ethic: An Exploration of Veganism*. The classic "why to" and "how to" book on adopting a vegan lifestyle. As valuable now as when it was first published.

Stepaniak, Joanne, *The Vegan Sourcebook and Being Vegan: Living with Conscience, Conviction, and Compassion*. Between them, these two books will tell you everything you need to know about vegan living. Gentle and down to earth, these beautifully written books will take the anxiety out of changing your lifestyle.

Vivisection

Ryder, Richard D., *Victims of Science*. Revised Edition. Dated, but still an outstanding introduction to the history and practice of vivisection.

WEBSITES/RESOURCES

Animal Rights

Note:

This is only a small sample of the many outstanding websites/organizations devoted to the protection of animals. These sites will lead you to others, and the omission of a site from this list should not be taken to mean that it is less helpful than the sites that are listed.

Compassion Over Killing: <www.cok.net> A local Washington, D.C. group that has gained a national reputation through its effective campaigns against the fur trade and factory farming and on behalf of a vegan lifestyle.

Doris Day Animal League: <www.ddal.org> Focused primarily on companion animal issues; other campaigns include horses and geese.

Farm Animal Reform Movement (FARM): <www.farmusa.org> Campaigns for a vegan lifestyle and against factory farming. Creator of the annual "Great American Meatout" and sponsor of the largest annual animal rights conference in North America.

Farm Sanctuary: <www.farmsanctuary.org> Operates two sanctuaries for rescued farmed animals and conducts national campaigns against factory farming and in support of a vegan lifestyle.

The Fund for Animals: <www.fund.org> The organization for which I work. An animal protection group founded in 1967 by author and humanitarian Cleveland Amory. The Fund focuses mainly on issues related to wildlife (hunting and trapping), animals in entertainment (circuses), and the fur trade, and operates several sanctuaries, including the 1,400-acre Black Beauty Ranch in Murchison, Texas.

The Humane Society of the United States: <www.hsus.org> The nation's largest animal protection group. In addition to their well-known companion animal campaigns, HSUS also works on wildlife, vivisection, and a variety of other issues.

In Defense of Animals (IDA): <www.idausa.org> Conducts national and international campaigns on behalf of companion animals.

Performing Animal Welfare Society (PAWS): <www.pawsweb.org>

Devoted to the protection of animals in entertainment: circuses, movies, etc.

People for the Ethical Treatment of Animals (PETA): <www.peta.org> The world's largest and best-known animal rights organization.

SHowing Animals Respect and Kindness (SHARK): <www.shark-online.org> Campaigns primarily against rodeos, bullfights, and hunting.

United Poultry Concerns: <www.upc-online.org> The only national animal rights group devoted exclusively to the protection of domestic fowl.

Vegetarian/Vegan Lifestyle

Note:
This is only a small sample of the many outstanding websites/organizations devoted to veganism and vegetarianism. These sites will lead you to others, and the omission of a site from this list should not be taken to mean that it is less helpful than the sites that are listed.

American Vegan Society: <www.americanvegan.org> Spiritually oriented website of the group founded by vegan pioneers Jay and Freya Dinshah. Information on a wide variety of vegan topics from ahimsa to health and the environment.

International Vegetarian Union (IVU): <www.ivu.org> Remarkably comprehensive website on all aspects of vegetarianism by the world's leading vegetarian advocacy and support group.

Joanne Stepaniak: <www.vegsource.com/joanne> Health, nutrition, and lifestyle information for vegans. Information about adopting a vegan lifestyle, Q's and A's, and essays on the spiritual aspects of veganism.

Dr. Michael Klaper: <www.vegsource.com/klaper> Health and nutrition information from a physician who has studied vegan nutrition for three decades.

North American Vegetarian Society (NAVS): <www.navs-online.org> Comprehensive website by North America's premier vegetarian organization and sponsor of the annual "Summerfest" vegetarian conference.

Physicians' Committee for Responsible Medicine (PCRM): <www.pcrm.org> Promotes a vegan lifestyle and opposes biomedical research on animals. Provides heath and nutrition information prepared by physicians and nutritionists.

Vegetarian Resource Group (VRG): <www.vrg.org> A wide array of authoritative health and nutrition information plus cooking tips and recipes.

Vegsource: <www.vegsource.com> "Vegetarian Central." Hosts multiple websites on vegetarianism/veganism relating to ethics, health, nutrition, cooking, and lifestyle.

The VivaVegie Society: <www.vivavegie.org> Health, nutrition, cooking, and lifestyle information.

Buddhism and Animals

Buddhist Resources on Vegetarianism and Animal Welfare
<http://online.sfsu.edu/~rone/Buddhism/BuddhismAnimalsVegetarian>, viewed February 9, 2004. Compiled by Ron Epstein, Philosophy Department, San Francisco State University. A wide-ranging collection of Buddhist texts, articles, and links. An excellent resource.

Meditate to Liberate—Spirituality and Animal Liberation
<www.meditatetoliberate.org.uk> A Buddhist organization based in the UK that campaigns for animal protection as a practice of engaged Buddhism. Their website features an informative interview with Dr. Tony Page, author of *Buddhism and Animals.*

Pakistan Vegetarian Society
<www.geocities.com/pakveg> Website contains several excellent articles, including "A Buddhist View of Vegetarianism" and "A Buddhist Perspective on Vegetarianism."

Society of Ethical and Religious Vegetarians (SERV)
<www.serv-online> An ecumenical group that advocates vegetarianism on the basis of the ethical teachings of the world's major religions. An excellent website features an extensive bibliography, a list of quotations, articles, and links.

Tara Project Australia
<http://ourworld.compuserve.com/homepages/TheTaraProjectAustralia>, viewed February 9, 2004. A Buddhist social service organization whose activities include projects to relieve animal suffering and prevent animal cruelty in Nepal. The Tara Project Australia, 6 Walter Street, Leichhardt, NSW 2046, Australia.

Universal Compassion Movement (UCM)
<www.universalcompassion.org> A Tibetan Buddhist organization founded and led by Geshe Thupten Phelgye to promote vegetarianism and conduct relief projects for both animals and humans. Geshe Thupten Phelgye, Universal Compassion Movement, Ahimsa House, MeLeod Ganj 176219, Dharamsala, H.P., India.

Periodicals

Animal People: <www.animalpeople.org> Published monthly in newspaper format. Extensive coverage of news of interest to animal advocates from North America and around the world.

Animals' Voice: <www.animalsvoice.com> Online animal rights magazine featuring articles, book reviews, and a large database of images of animal exploitation.

Satya: <www.satyamag.com> Essays, interviews, and book reviews dealing with animal advocacy, environmentalism, vegetarianism, and social justice.

VegNews: <www.vegnews.com> Published monthly. Contains news, think pieces, and book reviews on vegetarianism and animal rights.

BIBLIOGRAPHY

Adams, Carol J. *The Inner Art of Vegetarianism: Spiritual Practices for Body and Soul*. Lantern Books, New York, 2000.

———. *Living Among Meat Eaters: The Vegetarian's Survival Handbook*. Three Rivers Press, New York, 2001.

American Dietetic Association and Dietitians of Canada. "Position of the American Dietetic Association and Dietitians of Canada: Vegetarian Diets." *Journal of the American Dietetic Association*, Vol. 103, No. 6, June 2003.

Amey, Rosemary A. "Animal Rights and the Dhammapada." <www.rose-maryamey.com/dhamma>, viewed February 9, 2004.

Angulimala Sutta, the *Majjhima Nikaya*, 86, translated from the Pali by Thanissaro Bhikkhu. <www.accesstoinsight.org>.

"Animal Liberation Report" in *Vajrayana News*, March, 2002.

Armstrong, Karen. *Buddha*. Lipper/Viking, New York, 2001.

Ashoka. *The Edicts of King Ashoka: An English Rendering by Ven. S. Dhammika*. Buddhist Publication Society, Kandy, Sri Lanka, 1993.

Barber, Theodore Xenophon. *The Human Nature of Birds: A Scientific Discovery with Startling Implications*. St. Martin's Press, New York, 1993.

Bekoff, Marc. *Strolling with Our Kin: Speaking for and Respecting Voiceless Animals*. American Anti-Vivisection Society / Lantern Books, Jenkintown, Pennsylvania / New York, 2000.

———., Editor, *The Smile of a Dolphin: Remarkable Accounts of Animal Emotions*. Discovery Books / Random House, New York, 2000.

———. *Minding Animals: Awareness, Emotions, and Heart*. Oxford University Press, Oxford, 2002.

Bentham, Jeremy. *Introduction to the Principles of Morals and Legislation*. Hafner Press, New York, 1948.

Berry, Rynn. *Food for the Gods: Vegetarianism and the World's Religions*. Pythagorean Publishers, New York, 1998.

Braunstein, Mark Matthew. "Roadkill: Driving Animals to Their Graves." In *Animal Issues*, Vol. 29, No. 3, Fall 1998.

Carman, Judy. *Peace to All Beings: Veggie Soup for the Chicken's Soul*. Lantern Books, New York, 2003.

Cavalieri, Paola. *The Animal Question: Why Nonhuman Animals Deserve Human Rights.* Oxford University Press, Oxford, 2001.

Chapple, Christopher Key. *Nonviolence to Animals, Earth, and Self in Asian Traditions.* State University of New York Press, Albany, 1993.

Cleland, Trena. "Eating the Precepts: A Perspective." In *Turning Wheel: The Journal of Socially Engaged Buddhism,* Winter 2003–2004.

Clifton, Merritt. "Roadkill Avoidance Tips." In *Animal Issues,* Vol. 29, No. 3, Fall 1998.

Coetzee, J. M., et al. *The Lives of Animals,* edited by Amy Gutmann. Princeton University Press, Princeton, 1999.

Conze, Edward. *A Short History of Buddhism.* Oneworld Publications, Oxford, 1993.

The Dalai Lama (Tenzin Gyatso). *Freedom in Exile: The Autobiography of the Dalai Lama.* HarperCollins, New York, 1990.

———. *Beyond Dogma: Dialogues and Discourses.* North Atlantic Books, Berkeley, 1996.

———. *The Compassionate Life.* Wisdom Publications, Boston, 2001.

———. *Live in a Better Way: Reflections on Truth, Love, and Happiness,* compiled and edited by Renuka Singh. Viking Compass, New York, 2001.

———. *A Simple Path.* Thorsons, London, 2002.

The Dalai Lama and Fabien Ouaki. *Imagine All the People: A Conversation with the Dalai Lama on Money, Politics, and Life as It Could Be.* Wisdom Publications, Boston, 1999.

Davis, Karen. Prisoned Chickens, Poisoned Eggs: An Inside Look at the Modern Poultry Industry. Book Publishing Company, Summertown, Tennessee, 1997.

DeGrazia, David. *Animal Rights: A Very Short Introduction.* Oxford University Press, Oxford, 2001.

Deshung Rinpoche. *The Three Levels of Spiritual Perception,* translated by Jared Rhoton. Wisdom Publications, Boston, 1995.

The Dhammapada: The Path of Perfection, translated from the Pali with an introduction by Juan Mascaro. Penguin Books, London, 1973.

Dunayer, Joan. *Animal Equality: Language and Liberation.* Ryce Publishing, Derwood, Maryland, 2001.

Eisnitz, Gail A. *Slaughterhouse: The Shocking Story of Greed, Neglect, and Inhumane Treatment Inside the U.S. Meat Industry.* Prometheus Books, Amherst, New York, 1997.

The Encyclopedia of Eastern Philosophy and Religion. Shambhala Publications, Boston, 1989.

Farm Animal Reform Movement (FARM). "News of a Dying Industry: How Many Are Killed?" Bethesda, Maryland, 2002.

Gethin, Rupert. *The Foundations of Buddhism.* Oxford University Press, Oxford, 1998.

Goddard, Dwight, Editor. *A Buddhist Bible.* Beacon Press, Boston, 1994. (Originally published 1938.)

Goldstein, Joseph. *One Dharma: The Emerging Western Buddhism.* Harper-SanFrancisco, New York, 2002.

Goydon, Raymond, and Stephen Kindel. "Horse Slaughter: An Unnecessary Evil." The Thoroughbred Retirement Foundation, Inc. <www.trfinc.org>.

Green, Alan and the Center for Public Integrity. *Animal Underworld:Inside America's Black Market for Rare and Endangered Species.* Public Affairs, Washington, D.C., 1999.

Greyhound Protection League. <www.greyhounds.org>.

Gunaratana, Bhante Henepola. *Eight Steps to Mindfulness: Walking the Path of the Buddha.* Wisdom Publications, Boston, 2001.

Gyatso, Janet. *Apparitions of the Self: The Secret Autobiographies of a Tibetan Visionary.* Princeton University Press, Princeton, 1998.

Gyatso, Geshe Kelsang. *Universal Compassion.* Tharpa Publications, London, 1994.

Harvey, Peter. *An Introduction to Buddhism: Teachings, History, Practice.* Cambridge University Press, Cambridge, 1990.

———. *An Introduction to Buddhist Ethics.* Cambridge University Press, Cambridge, 2000.

Hendrickx, Marie. "Causing Animals Needless Suffering Is Contrary to Human Dignity." *L' Osservatore Romano,* Weekly Edition in English, January 24, 2001.

Humane Society of the United States (HSUS). "HSUS Pet Overpopulation Estimates." <www.hsus.org>.

Jamgon Kongtrul Lodro Thaye. *The Essence of Benefit and Joy: A Method for Saving Lives.* City Publications, Vancouver, 2000.

Jones, Lisa. "The Buckshot Bodhisattva: An Eco-Warrior Finds the Dharma, Opens His Heart, and Goes Hunting." *Tricycle: The Buddhist Review.* Number 50, Winter 2003.

Kain, John. "Eating Just the Right Amount." *Tricycle: The Buddhist Review,* Fall 2003.

Kalu Rinpoche. *The Dharma That Illuminates All Beings Impartially Like the Light of the Sun and the Moon.* State University of New York Press, Albany, 1986.

Kapleau, Philip. *To Cherish All Life: A Buddhist Case for Becoming Vegetarian.* The Zen Center, Rochester, New York, 1981.

Keown, Damien. *Buddhism and Bioethics.* Palgrave, London, 2001.

———. *A Dictionary of Buddhism.* Oxford University Press, Oxford, 2003.

Khetsun Sangpo Rinpoche. *Tantric Practice in Nyingma.* Snow Lion, Ithaca, New York, 1982.

Klaper, Michael. "Michael Klaper, M.D., Institute of Nutrition Education and Research" (website), <www.vegsource.com/klaper>, viewed February 9, 2004.

Knowles, Julie. "The Spiritual Universe: An Interview with Author Fred Alan Wolf." <http://twm.co.nz/wolf_int.html>, viewed February 9, 2004.

Kreisler, Kristin von. *The Compassion of Animals: True Stories of Animal Courage and Kindness.* Prima Publishing, Rocklin, California, 1997.

———. *Beauty in the Beasts: True Stories of Animals Who Choose to Do Good,* Jeremy C. Tarcher/Putnam, New York, 2001.

Landaw, Jonathan, and Andy Weber. *Images of Enlightenment: Tibetan Art in Practice.* Snow Lion Publications, Ithaca, New York, 1993.

The Lankavatara Sutra: A Mahayana Text, translated by D. T. Suzuki. Munshiram Manoharlal Publishers Pvt. Ltd., New Delhi, 1999.

Lawrence, Kate. "Nourishing Ourselves, Nourishing Others: How Mindful Food Choices Reduce Suffering." In *Mindfulness in the Marketplace: Compassionate Responses to Consumerism,* edited by Allan Hunt Badiner. Parallax Press, Berkeley, 2002.

Lewis, C. S. *The Problem of Pain.* HarperCollins, New York, 2001.

Linden, Eugene. *The Parrot's Lament: And Other True Tales of Animal Intrigue, Intelligence, and Ingenuity.* The Penguin Group, New York, 1999.

———. *The Octopus and the Orangutan: New Tales of Animal Intrigue, Intelligence, and Ingenuity.* The Penguin Group, New York, 2002.

Lyman, Howard F., with Glen Merzer. *Mad Cowboy: Plain Truth from the Cattle Rancher Who Won't Eat Meat.* Scribner, New York, 1998.

The Long Discourses of the Buddha: A Translation of the Digha Nikaya, translated from the Pali by Maurice Walshe. Wisdom Publications, Boston, 1996.

Marcus, Eric. *Vegan: The New Ethics of Eating.* Revised Edition. McBooks Press, Ithaca, New York, 2000.

Mason, Jim, and Peter Singer. *Animal Factories* (revised and updated). Harmony Books, New York, 1990.

Masson, Jeffrey Moussaieff. *The Pig Who Sang to the Moon: The Emotional World of Farm Animals.* Ballantine Books, New York, 2003.

Masson, Jeffrey Moussaieff, and Susan McCarthy. *When Elephants Weep: The Emotional Lives of Animals.* Delacourt Press, New York, 1995.

The Middle Length Discourses of the Buddha: A Translation of the Majjhima Nikaya, translated from the Pali by Bhikkhu Nanamoli and Bhikkhu Bodhi. Wisdom Publications, Boston, 1995.

Moran, Victoria. *Compassion, The Ultimate Ethic: An Exploration of Veganism.* Thorsons Publishers Limited, Wellingborough, UK, 1985.

Narada, Mahathera. *The Buddha and His Teachings,* Second Revised and Enlarged Edition. Buddhist Publication Society, Kandy, Sri Lanka, 1988.

National Agricultural Statistical Service, U.S. Department of Agriculture. "Agricultural Statistics Data Base: U.S. and State Data," <www.nass.usda.gov>.

National Anti-Vivisection Society (NAVS). "NAVS: Credible Answers for a Cruelty-Free World," <http://www.navs.org>.

Nhat Hanh, Thich. *Interbeing: Fourteen Guidelines for Engaged Buddhism.* Revised Edition. Parallax Press, Berkeley, 1987.

———. *Old Path, White Clouds: Walking in the Footsteps of the Buddha.* Parallax Press, Berkeley, 1991.

———. *Touching Peace: Practicing the Art of Mindful Living.* Parallax Press, Berkeley, 1992.

———. *Love in Action: Writings on Nonviolent Social Change.* Parallax Press, Berkeley, 1993.

———. *Stepping into Freedom: An Introduction to Buddhist Monastic Training.* Parallax Press, Berkeley, 1997.

———., et al., *For a Future to be Possible: Commentaries on the Five Mindfulness Trainings.* Revised Edition. Parallax Press, Berkeley, 1998.

Page, Tony, *Buddhism and Animals: A Buddhist Vision of Humanity's Rightful Relationship with the Animal Kingdom.* UKAVIS Publications (United Kingdom Anti-Vivisection Information Society), London, 1999.

Patrul Rinpoche, *The Words of My Perfect Teacher.* HarperCollins, San Francisco, 1994.

Patterson, Charles, *Eternal Treblinka: Our Treatment of Animals and the Holocaust.* Lantern Books, New York, 2002.

Phelps, Norm, "A Dying Sport: The State of Hunting in America." The Fund for Animals, New York, 2004.

Rabten, Geshe, *The Essential Nectar: Meditations on the Buddhist Path.* Wisdom Publications, Boston, 1984.

Rahula, Walpola, *What the Buddha Taught.* Gordon Fraser Gallery Ltd., London, 1978.

———. *The Heritage of the Bhikkhu: The Buddhist Tradition of Service.* Grove Press, New York, 1974.

Randour, Mary Lou. *Animal Grace: Entering a Spiritual Relationship with Our Fellow Creatures.* New World Library, Novato, California, 2000.

Ray, Reginald, *Indestructible Truth: The Living Spirituality of Tibetan Buddhism.* Shambhala Publications, Boston, 2000.

Regan, Tom, *The Case for Animal Rights.* University of California Press, Berkeley, 1983.

———.*Empty Cages: Facing the Challenge of Animal Rights.* Rowman and Littlefield Publishers, Inc., Lanham, Maryland, 2004.

Rosen, Steven, *Diet for Transcendence: Vegetarianism and the World's Religions.* Torchlight Publishing, Badger, California, 1997.

Saddhatissa, Hammalawa, *Buddhist Ethics.* Third Edition. Wisdom Publications, Boston, 1997.

Schumann, H. W., *The Historical Buddha: The Life, Times, and Teachings of the Founder of Buddhism, translated from the German by M. O'C. Walshe.* Arkana, London, 1989.

Scully, Matthew, *Dominion: The Power of Man, the Suffering of Animals, and the Call to Mercy.* St. Martin's Press, New York, 2002.

Shabkar (Shabkar Tsogdruk Rangdrol), *The Life of Shabkar: The Autobiography of a Tibetan Yogin,* with a foreword by H.H. the Dalai Lama, translated by Matthieu Ricard. Snow Lion Publications, Ithaca, New York, 2001.

The Shambhala Dictionary of Buddhism and Zen, translated by Michael H. Kohn from *Lexikon der oestlichen Weisheitslehren* by Ingrid Fischer-Schreiber, Franz-Karl Ehrhard, and Michael S. Diener. Shambhala Publications, Boston, 1991.

Smith, Jean, *The Beginner's Guide to Walking the Buddha's Eightfold Path.* Bell Tower, New York, 2002.

Snelling, John, *The Buddhist Handbook: The Complete Guide to Buddhist Schools, Teaching, Practice, and History.* Inner Traditions International, Rochester, Vermont, 1991.

Sogyal Rinpoche, *The Tibetan Book of Living and Dying.* HarperSanFrancisco, New York, 1992.

Stallwood, Kim W., Editor, *A Primer on Animal Rights: Leading Experts Write About Animal Cruelty and Exploitation.* Lantern Books, New York, 2002.

Stepaniak, Joanne, *The Vegan Sourcebook,* McGraw-Hill, New York, 2000.

———.*Being Vegan: Living with Conscience, Conviction, and Compassion,* Lowell House, Los Angeles, 2000.

Stevenson, Ian, *Twenty Cases Suggestive of Reincarnation.* University of Virginia Press, Charlottesville, 1974.

Surya Das, "Do Buddhists Have to Give Up Sex, Meat, and Alcohol?" Beliefnet, <www.beliefnet.com/story/1/story_178.html>, viewed February 9, 2004.

Thurman, Robert A. F., *Inner Revolution: Life, Liberty, and the Pursuit of Real Happiness.* Penguin Putnam, Inc., New York, 1998.

Tobias, Michael, and Kate Solisti-Mattelon, Editors, *Kinship with the Animals.* Beyond Words Publishing, Hillsboro, Oregon, 1998.

Tworkov, Helen, Editor, "Meat: To Eat It or Not: A Debate on Food and Practice." In *Tricycle: The Buddhist Review,* Vol. 4, No. 2, Winter 1994.

Waldau, Paul, *The Specter of Speciesism: Buddhist and Christian Views of Animals.* Oxford University Press, Oxford, 2002.

Zimmer, Heinrich, *Philosophies of India,* edited by Joseph Campbell. Princeton University Press, Princeton, 1989. (Originally published in 1951.)

Zopa Rinpoche, *Ultimate Healing: The Power of Compassion.* Wisdom Publications, Boston, 2001.

Of Related Interest From Lantern Books

The Dominion of Love
Animal Rights According to the Bible
Norm Phelps

"After decades of neglect, churches are beginning to take the issue of justice to animals seriously. Many books have influenced this change, and *The Dominion of Love* is an insightful, judicious, and inspiring contribution to this growing library."
—The Rev. Dr. Andrew Linzey, Oxford University; author, *Animal Theology*

Holy Cow
The Hare Krishna Contribution to Vegetarianism and Animal Rights
Steven J. Rosen

Unlocks the philosophy of compassion for all living entities that informs the Hare Krishna movement's vegetarian practices and defense of animal rights.
"A universally sound, non-sectarian guide for all true seekers."
—Chrissie Hynde

Judaism and Vegetarianism
New Revised Edition
Richard H. Schwartz, Ph.D.

"In his scholarly and thoughtful style, Richard Schwartz demonstrates the profound imperatives at the heart of the Jewish faith that lead inexorably in a vegetarian direction."—**John Robbins**, author, *Diet for a New America*

God's Covenant With Animals
A Biblical Basis for the Humane Treatment of All Creatures
J. R. Hyland

"[Hyland] speaks with great authority, combining scholarship and passion with a prophetic voice."—**Stephen H. Webb**, author, *On God and Dogs*

The Bible According to Noah
Theology as if Animals Mattered
Gary Kowalski

Kowalski explores the ancient stories of the Bible to examine their relevance today—especially in regard to how we view and treat other animals.
"Kowalski offers religious communities an example, based on both knowledge of scripture and of the spirit, of how to treat animals with the dignity they deserve."
—**Mary Lou Randour**, author, *Animal Grace*

The Lost Religion of Jesus
Simple Living and Nonviolence in Early Christianity
Keith Akers

Akers argues that Jewish Christianity was vegetarian and practiced pacifism and communal living.
"A whole new conception of Christianity."—**Walter Wink**

The Inner Art Trilogy
Spiritual Practices for Body and Soul
Carol J. Adams

Including:
The Inner Art of Vegetarianism
The Inner Art of Vegetarianism Workbook
Meditations on the Inner Art of Vegetarianism

An exploration of the inner life of vegetarianism and the outer life of compassion in action.

The Green Bible
Stephen Bede Scharper, Hilary Cunningham

"A book of inspiration and transformation for the green-minded, and for those who wish to be or should be."—**Matthew Fox**

Animal Equality
Language and Liberation
Joan Dunayer

"Animal Equality establishes speciesism and language as a field of study while providing the benchmark for the field."
—**Carol J. Adams**, author of *The Sexual Politics of Meat*
"Brilliant and devastating."—**Tom Regan**

Eternal Treblinka
Our Treatment of Animals and the Holocaust
Charles Patterson, Ph.D.
Foreword by Lucy Rosen Kaplan, Esq.

"Charles Patterson's book will go a long way towards righting the terrible wrongs that human beings, throughout history, have perpetrated on non-human animals. I urge you to read it and think deeply about its important message."—**Jane Goodall**

More Than a Meal
The Turkey in Myth, History, Ritual, and Tradition
Karen Davis, Ph.D.

Davis examines how our treatment of turkeys and other animals shapes our other values, our relationship with other human beings, and our attitude toward the land, nation, and the world. "Shines a new light on the unfortunate, much-maligned bird."
—**Peter Singer**

A Primer on Animal Rights
Leading Experts Write about Animal Cruelty and Exploitation
Kim Stallwood

Articles that document how animals are cruelly mistreated and commercially exploited for profit.

Strolling with Our Kin
Speaking for and Respecting Voiceless Animals
Marc Bekoff
Foreword by Jane Goodall

Bekoff takes the reader on a philosophical and ethical odyssey examining how we can all live in harmony with our fellow kin. "A major inspiration."—*Journal of Agricultural and Environmental Sciences*

The Way of Compassion
Vegetarianism, Environmentalism, Animal Advocacy, and Social Justice
Martin Rowe, Editor

"This eloquent, forceful body of writings ... forges vital links between vegetarianism, environmentalism and animal rights and the quest for social justice."—*Publishers Weekly*

To Order:
Call 1.800.856.8664 or visit www.lanternbooks.com

CPSIA information can be obtained
at www.ICGtesting.com
Printed in the USA
FFHW02n1202250918